Days Long Gone

Days Long Gone

Memories of Threshing and Sawmilling with Steam Engines in Herefordshire & Radnorshire

by

David L.T. Price

Logaston Press

LOGASTON PRESS
Little Logaston Woonton Almeley
Herefordshire HR3 6QH
logastonpress.co.uk

First published by Logaston Press 2011
Copyright © David L.T. Price 2011

All rights reserved. No part of this publication
may be reproduced, stored in a retrieval system,
or transmitted, in any form or by any means,
electronic, mechanical, photocopying, recording
or otherwise, without the prior permission,
in writing, of the publisher

ISBN 978 1 906663 58 2

Typeset by Logaston Press
and printed and bound in Malta
by Gutenberg Press

Contents

	Preface	*vii*
1	My Family and Steam	1
2	Father's First World War Memories	27
3	Threshing, Sawing and other work	35
4	Stories round the fire	95
	Appendix	113

Preface

I hope you will enjoy these stories. I have told them all as they were related to me. I have still got a lot of stories that my father told me of his experiences with engines over the years. Most of them are written down, but whether they will ever be printed I don't know. Of late I have had a lot of trouble with my eyes, and can't read for long now.

It was indeed a wonderful experience to be involved in the last days of steam. It was very sad to see it all disappear, and a way of life never to be seen again.

Most of the photos are from my father's collection; some were given to him years ago, but a few have been given to me.

I would like to say thank you to all the folks who have given me work over the years, and took the time and trouble to speak to me so that I could lip-read them.

The Dear Old Shop

I will go down to the shop once more,
the dear old shop of my youth.
Where once the forge did roar,
and hammers rang with mighty blows from mighty thews,
as upon the anvil the red hot iron bent,
from forces greater still than thou.
The bellows rattled, the sparks did fly,
the anvil rang, the water sizzled.
The task was done.

But now the forge is cold and stilled,
the bellows breathed its last.
The hammers upon the silent anvil rest,
as rust and dust collect.

In the dear old shop the men of years ago
no longer ply their trade.
All is still and silent and quiet as the grave.
But in the Church Yard they are sleeping,
beneath the tower great and strong,
for their work on earth is done.
And for ever more they rest.
Oh, will we meet again to talk of old, old days.
Of days of strife and struggle.
Of days of bliss and happiness.
Of days of sorrow, tears and toil,
and partings sad recalled.

But ah, we shall meet again,
when all the tears are wiped away.
Oh what joy sublime and smiles upon our countenances glow,
when at the Saviour's feet we sit.
To be for ever blessed
with Peace and Health and Happiness.

1 My Family and Steam

My family had lived in a house called Pentrejack since 1757, a house which lies in the spread out village of Brilley in north-west Herefordshire on the border with Wales, and a house which they bought in 1772 for £35. It was here that my great grandfather, the Old Man as we called him, lived, and it was here that his first wife died shortly after giving birth to my grandfather, Papa Price. Papa Price could remember his grandfather, the Old Man's father, sat on a bench outside the door of Pentrejack wearing something like a black top hat. This must have been going back 200 years or so.

Pentrejack. The wooden building was the carpenter's shop where all the coopering and other carpentry was carried out. Behind the stable door was the stable for the pony and a pigscot, above which was a hayloft. The blacksmith's shop with a forge and lathe has since been knocked down.

The house once contained a secret room upstairs to which the opening had been sealed off. When I carried out some repairs to the roof some years past, having removed the tiles from over the room, I was able to look down into the interior of it and saw a baby's cradle there. They used to put the babies in this room to sleep, as being near to the chimney it was warm. The room has since been opened up and the cradle removed.

Pentrejack had just a couple of acres and the Old Man, Papa Price and, in due course, my father, all earned their living through a variety of threshing and sawing. The Old Man had been a cooper, but trade was falling off and when reading the Bible one evening came across Genesis chapter 8 verse 22: 'While the earth remaineth, seedtime and harvest, and cold and heat, and summer and winter, and day and night shall not cease' and so formed the idea of a threshing business which would be required year after year. Thus he established a business operating a variety of steam powered machinery and undertaking, in the main, threshing and saw milling jobs across a swathe of north-west Herefordshire and into Radnorshire as far as Penybont. Father's threshing work would commence in the autumn at Moccas in

Going threshing in the snow circa 1892. Papa Price, then aged about 21, is the engine driver wearing the bowler hat. The engine is called Daisy Bell and might be a Marshall.

Papa Price at work on a sawing job around 1894. In the top photograph he is standing in front of the hind wheel holding an oil can. In the lower photograph the man standing by the pile of timber is holding a pattern for wooden wheels to be cut on the bandsaw.

One of the Old Man's engines, a Clayton and Shuttleworth of 1865, no.1340. The smoke box carried on up round the cylinder. The photo was taken in 1935 at the home of my uncle Maurice Price in Llowes.

the Wye valley, and worked his way up towards Presteigne and then west past Old and New Radnor to farms near Knighton and Penybont, with the work carrying on over the winter and even into the following spring. The sawmilling work was usually carried out on a contract basis. A semi-permanent base would be established in the woodland, with a covered sawmill and a cabin in which to live during the week, the woodland being worked over a number of years. But sometimes there would be work at a wood for just the one season, when they might choose to sleep in a van that they had rather than erect a cabin.

They also had a blacksmith's and carpenter's shop at Pentrejack where they could repair their own and others' machinery, especially during the summer months. Within a few years there came to be so much tack in that yard, you could hardly move. There were many old threshing drums and portable engines including a portable forge on wheels that the Old Man could take round the yard from job to job while repairing the tack. It saved a lot of walking back and forth to the blacksmith's shop.

In later years, when threshing and sawing work dropped off, my father and uncle carried out some well digging and laying pipes for water supply.

The Old Man didn't remain a widower for too long and on the day that he was to get married for the second time he was threshing at a farm above the church. Threshing and work was all important to him, he could not stop work and lose a whole day's threshing just to get married. As the hour drew near to tie the knot, he knocked off work and made his way out of the rickyard towards the church, no doubt watched by all the men. He was still in his working clothes – corduroy trousers, yorks at the knees and covered with dust – but he changed into his best clothes in a hut in a nearby wood.

Having got married, he made a stop in the same place to change back into his working clothes and then returned to the rickyard to get on with his threshing. Why, you could not lose a full day's threshing for a little event like getting married! Some farmers, on hearing that the Old Man changed his clothes in this wood on his wedding day, named it CWM Thomas Wood after him. The Old Man had two sons through this second marriage, Gwyn and Maurice, who would be my great step uncles.

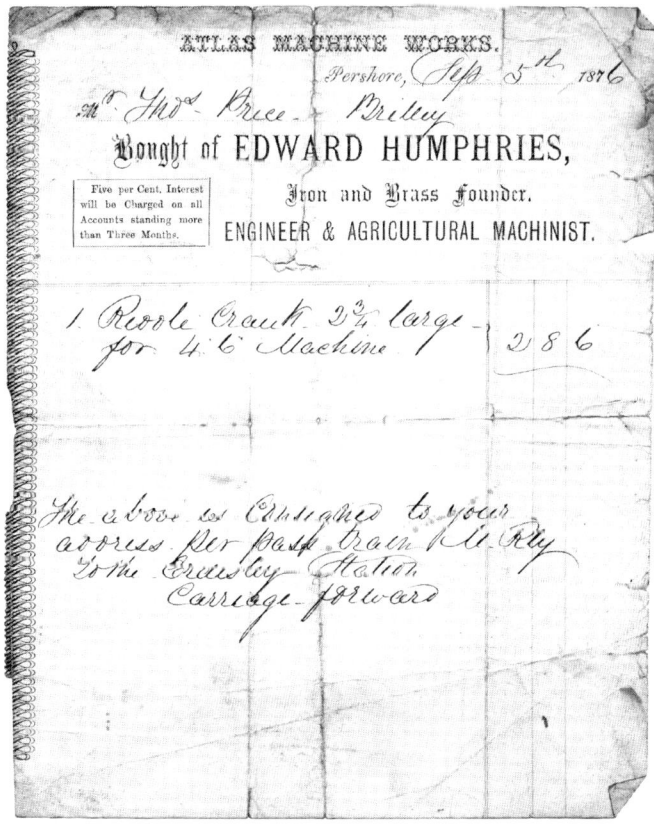

A bill made out in 1876 to the Old Man for parts for his threshing machine, with goods to be collected from Eardisley station.

The Old Man used to provide the food for the pig and the flour to bake the bread. He then gave his first wife £1 a week to cover all the other housekeeping. But as his new wife spent a lot of time away from home looking after sick people, and there was no supper or fire for him on getting home on cold dark winter nights after a hard day's threshing and a walk home of several miles, he cut it down to ten shillings.

The Old Man was very fussy about his work indeed, and would not let anyone distract him from putting his best efforts into the simplest of jobs, even temporary work. Once he was repairing a broken cast iron rainwater gutter at Llanhedry Farm by wrapping a piece of sheet iron round the gutter and riveting it on. He was making a tidy job of it as usual when the farmer who was watching said, 'There's no need to be so fussy on a little job like that, Mr. Price.'

Whereupon the Old Man replied, 'You never know who is going to look at it.'

He was still running his threshing machinery in 1910 when in his early 70s. It was a year when people in Brilley could smell that something was burning, but couldn't trace the source of it. Eventually it was found that a beam was smouldering in the church, and the Old Man was fetched from his threshing machine which was in the vicinity. Nothing daunted, he went up a ladder to the beam and sawed it through to help prevent the fire spreading from the church tower, which was destroyed, to the nave. While he was sawing the beam he noticed that the gap between the beam and the pipe from the church's stove was less than two inches, and this was the cause of the fire.

Brilley Church showing the wooden tower (top) that was burned down on 19 January 1910, and the damage caused by the fire.

I recall Father telling me that the church tower was carried on four huge stones at each corner of the building. Resting on top of these stones were four oak posts of great size ascending up into the tower itself. The bell or bells that were in the tower melted in the heat and the brass was splattered on the floor. After the fire people who visited the church to see for themselves the damage that had been caused, started picking up pieces of brass and taking them home as souvenirs, until this was stopped.

At one time the walls inside the church were painted over all with a kind of flower. Father more than once described these flowers and the colours to me, drawing pictures in the air with his hands as he recalled it to mind.

One amusing thing that he related to me was that a certain door in the church had a picture of a face painted on it. It was not a very nice picture as it looked somewhat like the devil, and the parson of the day painted it over in order to cover it up. Having got the first coat of paint on to his satisfaction, and no doubt thinking it was a job well done, to his dismay when the paint dried out the face showed through. So he painted over it again, and again it showed through. He painted it a third time and it was still showing. It became quite a joke in the parish with the people saying that the parson can't get rid of the devil. However, after several more coats of paint he managed to obliterate the face altogether.

One day when the parson went into the school to see the children he had some difficulty in getting over to them who Jesus Christ was. So he said to them, 'If all the people in Brilley were sheep, what would I be?'

One little boy put his hand up and said 'Please Sir, the Tup'.

Father on the left, Aunty Ciss and Uncle Idris.

In around 1895, Papa Price, the Old Man's son by his first marriage, married Granny Price – we named our relatives with a certain simplicity – who produced the next generation of my father, the eldest of three offspring, the others being my uncle Idris and my aunt Ciss.

As a young girl Granny Price lived with her parents, brothers and sisters at the Cwm farm above Llangorse Lake. The Cwm house and farm buildings are now no longer standing and the farm itself has been incorporated into another farm.

The school she went to was on the other side of the lake from her home, and when the lake froze over in the winter she was able to walk to school across the lake on the ice. But she always returned home after school by way of the road. She could remember on one occasion watching a team of horses hauling a timber carriage over the frozen lake.

Her father once had a contract to carry out some drainage work by the lake and while they were digging out the drainage trenches they came upon some lintels which appeared to be the tops of some door openings. Also they found a hole about the size of a small well. The hole disappeared straight down into the bowels of the earth and as they were unable to discern the bottom, they joined together three of the longest hazel wands that they could find, having a total length of approximately twenty to twenty-five feet. After lowering them down the opening they were unable to feel the bottom, whereupon they gave up. I have often wondered what these lintels were. Were they part of the drowned village that was reputed to be there?

A degree of mystery surrounds Granny Price. Some time in the late 1940s we were all going for a ride down to Llangorse Lake one afternoon and I was sat in the back between granny and Aunty Edie from Talgarth. As we motored along in Father's 1936 Morris, granny was pointing out the landmarks to me. 'You see that tower over there?' she said, pointing to Tretower Castle. 'It was on top of that tower that I made up my mind to go to Australia. A friend and myself were on top of the tower viewing the countryside and thinking how big the world was and what a lot there was to see. So we decided to go to Australia. But she never came with me.'

'What did you do then?' I asked.

'I went by myself,' she replied. 'My friend dropped out at the last minute.'

'Gosh', I said, 'she let you down badly there.'

'Yes,' she replied, 'and just before we docked on reaching Australia I had all my money stolen. So I arrived in Australia penniless.'

I was awestruck that such a calamity as arriving in a faraway country with no friends and no money should befall anyone. 'Whatever did you do then?'

'Oh, I went to the Captain and explained to him what had happened. Certain arrangements were made,' she replied.

'How old were you then?'

'Twenty-one,' she replied promptly, but I have reason to believe that she was younger than this.

'And why did you go, leaving all your family and friends?' I asked her.

'Adventure, David, I wanted to see the world, to travel and have adventure. To see what was the other side of the mountain.'

She must have been a brave young woman to have embarked on such an adventure in that day and age of 1883 or 1886 without friends or family to support her. I believe she made the outward journey aboard a sailing ship – she did tell me how long the journey took and I think it was something over six weeks.

Granny Price and her brother, Uncle Tom, who spent a long time in the Navy. The photo appears to be taken outside the front door of the Cooper's Cottage.

She eventually found work in the outback in Queensland.

'I was once going down to the river for a bucket of water,' she told me on another occasion when I was in her cottage, 'and as I drew near to the water a crocodile came straight for me. I took off, running for dear life, zig-zagging as I went.'

'How far was it behind you?' I asked.

'Oh I don't know, David,' replied Granny, 'I didn't stop until I got back to the farm. I just kept going for all I was worth. It was an awful fright to see it with its horrible mouth coming for me.' I was trying to picture in my mind Granny as a young girl in the outback running for her life with a crocodile snapping at her heels. But try as I might I just could not visualize this old and frail Granny of mine being chased by a crocodile.

'Why did you run zig-zag?' I asked her.

'I'd overheard the men and the hands talking about it,' she replied.

'Another time,' continued Granny, 'we were all sat down round the table having dinner. Just then I could feel something going over my bare feet. I looked under the table and I could see a snake crawling over my feet. So I sat very still and quiet, hardly breathing, not saying anything to the others. When it had passed on from me and was still crawling under the table, I still did not say anything to the others as I was afraid that they would jump up and frighten it into striking. When it had crawled some distance from the table I said, "Look, there is a snake over there." The men went out to get their sticks to kill it. By the time they had come back in, the snake had gone up in the rafters of the roof and the men had to get it down with a long stick that was kept for this purpose before killing and skinning it. And here is the skin,' said Granny, getting up from her chair and picking up a round leather box off the Welsh dresser. She removed the lid and lifted out the snake skin which was coiled up inside. 'The colours used to be very pretty, but they have faded.' I think she called it a sidewinder.

'We used to have some chickens about the yard and if there was a snake in the vicinity the chickens would set up a terrible din. When one of these snakes caught a chicken and coiled itself round the chicken's body you could hear the bones cracking as it squeezed the chicken to death.'

'Go on, Granny,' I said 'Never.'

'Yes, yes David, I have seen and heard it myself. It must have been an awful death for the chicken.'

After coiling up the snake skin and putting it back in the box which was returned to the dresser, she went on to tell me how she came by the coral from the Great Barrier Reef and the great sea-snail shell, both of them residing with the snake skin on the Welsh dresser as a reminder of her happy days in Australia.

She often remarked to me how happy she was out there, how free she felt, totally different from her life in England. She used to say to me how at one time before she met Papa Price and became his wife, she was going to return to Australia. 'But

Papa Price came along and I shall never go back now, David. I would like to see my first husband's grave once more, but I am too old to travel now, and it's too far away.'

Whilst in Queensland she met and married her first husband, but her adventurous life on the other side of the world was suddenly terminated by his death when he was caught and drowned in a flash flood as he was going to a silver mine on business. They would not let her see his body as it was some time before they found him and it was in a bad state from the heat and the dingos. He lies buried not far from where they found him and she had some iron railings put round his grave as a protection.

He left her with one very young child and a babe in arms with whom she returned to England. These two children, Harry and

Papa Price and Harry Turner, his stepson, in the yard with the Roby on which they had been carrying out some repairs.

Uncle Harry Turner and his wife Mabel on their wedding day. On the left in the back row are Granny and Papa Price; in the front row second from the left is Aunty Ciss.

The old Marshall outside its home at Pentrejack. The chimney once had to be cut off when on the road in order to get under a railway bridge. The Old Man purchased the Marshall and licensed it for work in Radnorshire; being the first traction engine licenced in the county, it was given the number 1. He was also the first man in Brilley to own a steam engine (this was an early portable engine). Papa Price, however, drove the engine more than anyone else and was the one to ask about it. Not being fitted with a differential, the Marshall was very awkward to move in tight places, and to move the tack involved many a taking out and putting back in of the drive pins. The front axle was later moved further back under the boiler to improve the handling. Over the years the winding drum under the boiler was removed and a cab was fitted, to be replaced by a second cab when that fell apart. When the main cog wheel needed replacing after it had become badly worn and many of its teeth had broken off, Gwyn had a new cast iron wheel made by Naylors in Hereford. Naylors made a full size pattern of one quarter of the wheel, pressing this into the sand four times to make the full cast. Gwyn reboxed the engine in the 1930s. Father said it was a most uncomfortable engine on which to ride as it was unsprung and you could feel your teeth rattling in your head and your eyeballs would be all of a quiver. The steersman stood behind the flywheel and also received the full draught from it. In addition, as the rim of the flywheel was very close to the back wheel, any clods of mud picked up by the back wheel were sprayed out by the flywheel and spattered the steersman with a straight line of mud down the middle of his hat, nose, lips and clothes. It was around 1918, sometime after the Old Man died, that Gwyn returned to live at Pentrejack, having been looking after a flour mill engine at Silverstone.

Another view of the old Marshall in the yard at Pentrejack in about 1919. On the footplate are Gwyn's two sons George and Sid. Below them is the draw bar, and to the left the threshing machine shakers with their hinges instead of a crankshaft to carry them.

Lil Turner, became part of our family too, Harry often working with my father.

The Old Man also owned a small cottage up the hill from Pentrejack, and known variously over the years as Coopers Cottage, Coopers By Tack and, much later, Hillside. The cottage was in a very bad state of repair and at one time only the two gable ends were left standing. Sometime between 1875 and 1900, the

The Marshall on Brilley Mountain, not far from a house called Summer Pole. On the footplate is Maurice Price. Behind him is the Old Man, and standing holding the flag is John Pugh, who also acted as the feeder on the threshing drum. The framework on the engine shows that the Old Man was making a new cab: the first one fell apart as he made it with screws which were shaken loose, so he used nuts and bolts on the new one. To the right of John Pugh's elbow can just be discerned the Radnorshire licence plate with the number 1.

The Marshall engine during the First World War. Sat on the extension bracket on the front is the Old Man, then at least in his late 70s, with his back to the smoke box to help him keep warm. Papa Price is driving and Uncle Idris is steering (my father was then in the army in France). Behind the Old Man is the draw bar tied to the chimney stump.

The old Marshall in use as a ploughing engine.

Old Man, with the help of the Old Lady, his wife, carried out some work, rebuilding the front in brick to prevent the old cottage collapsing altogether. It was here that Papa and Granny Price came to live, erecting a further blacksmith's and carpenter's shop in the yard. Father used to say how busy they always were, turning, drilling, making fire boxes and fitting them, casting bearings, making smoke boxes and chimneys, boring cylinders, making wooden wheels and tyring them, re-shoeing the back wheels on the engine, re-tubing the boiler, balancing the drum, drilling out stay pins, cutting threads, making patterns for castings, riveting, making tools, sawing timber for repairs to the waggons and painting. It seems that painting was an awful job when carried out in the open. He said you did not want a breath of wind as the paint did not dry for three or four days and if a bit of wind came up and blew some dust on your work, the finish was spoilt. Or if you had a few spots of rain to splash on freshly painted work, the spots turned blue.

One day when Granny Price was at home at Coopers Cottage going about her duties as a wife and mother, one of the young children from Kintley Barn across the fields suddenly burst in upon her shouting in great consternation 'Come quick, Dad's hung himself.'

With great presence of mind Granny grabbed a kitchen knife and took off with the young child, running across the fields to Kintley Barn which must be well over 500 yards away. Entering the barn and seeing that the man was hanging from a rope by the neck, she cut him down and saved his life.

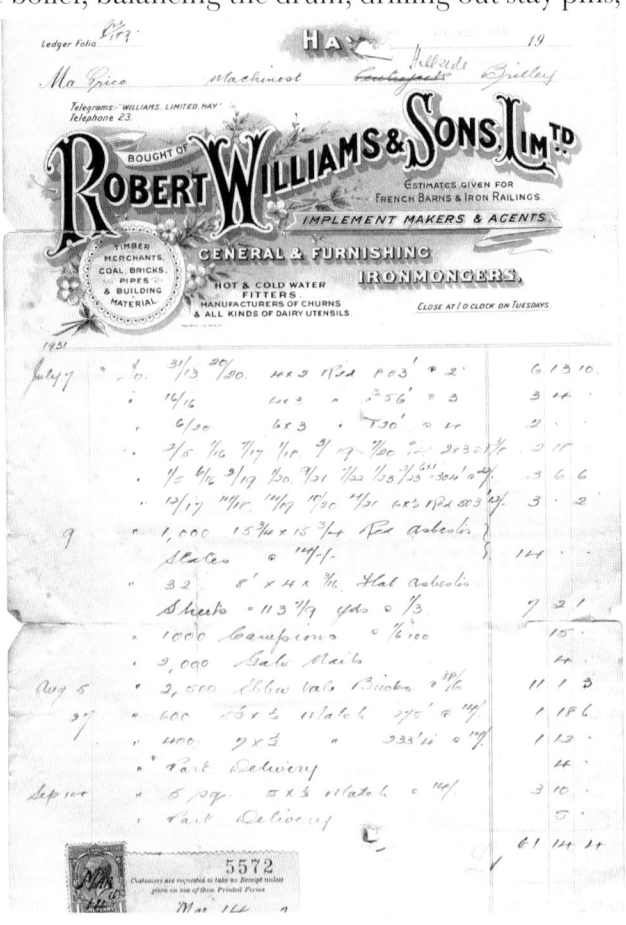

A bill for materials for the bungalow built by my father. He was owed £100 for some work he had carried out, on the strength of which he ordered the materials and started to build the bungalow in 1929-30. However, the man who owed him the money went bankrupt, and Father only managed to pay the bill 12 months later. Robert Williams & Sons remarked that he had taken a long time paying the bill, to which Father replied 'If you had some of my customers you would always be a long time getting paid.'

Father's loyal worker Wethersbrey working on the bungalow. The two girls are Father's nieces. My parents spent their honeymoon at his sister's house in London, near which was Perryn Road, after which he named the bungalow Perryn. He designed the bungalow so that the four corners faced the four points of the compass.

My sister, May.

This sorry state of affairs had a happy ending. The man had got into some sort of difficulties and it came to the hearing of certain people who offered or found him a job in another locality which he took and got on well. He said afterwards that the best thing he ever did was to hang himself!

In 1929-30 my father started to build a bungalow on a plot of land above Cooper's Cottage. This would provide a home for his family, my sister May who was born in 1931 and myself who was born in 1939. At the age of 16 May left home and went to work in London, eventually moving to the States.

The winter of 1947 has lived long in many memories, not least in ours. This one evening Father had walked the five hundred yards up the lane to the top road to go to Bill Bufton's, the roadman's house, to get the bread, it being the nearest house to which the baker could deliver the bread for ourselves and our neighbours. So bad were the conditions that at one time Father, Mother and several others had to walk the five miles into Kington and back for food supplies. At one place, I believe it was the pitch above Empton Pool, the snow had drifted so high across and over the road that it formed an overhead bridge and they had to walk through a tunnel underneath it, but the tunnel was only a yard or so in length.

Meanwhile, on the night in question, while Father went for the bread, Mother went down to the cottage to check that Papa and Granny were alright for the night, not stopping long that evening as I think she had had enough of the adverse winter conditions. So Mother, my sister and I were in the bungalow keeping warm sat by the fire of the cooking range. Mother was reading with the aid of the light from a candle which was resting on the top of the drop down oven door of the range.

Papa Price with the Fowler sawing in the yard at Perryn. Note the jack to steady the engine. At one time he used to drive an engine for Hereford Brick Works and once delivered some bricks to the Boat Inn in Whitney – but the work took him far and wide.

All of a sudden, 'Shhhh, be quiet, what's that noise?' asked Mother.

All was quiet, so we settled back down by the fire. Suddenly Mother said, 'I thought I heard the bell.' This bell was only rung at meal times to summon any men who were at work in the shop down to their meals at the cottage. If it was rung at any other time it meant that there was something seriously the matter which should be investigated without delay, and it was strictly forbidden for me or anyone else to ring the bell for any other reason.

'Yes, there it is', she said getting up from her chair, 'I can hear the tolling of a bell, something is wrong down below.' (The cottage was very often referred to as down below). Picking up the candle we hurried to the door just in time to see Papa arriving on the door-step ringing the bell.

'Whatever is the matter Papa?' asked mother. 'Has Granny fallen down?'

Granny and Papa Price in the autumn of their lives.

'No the beam's on fire!' said Papa, 'and the fire is roaring in the chimney. Where is Lew?' (short for Llewellyn, my father).

'Oh my gosh', said mother, putting her hand to her mouth. 'Lew's gone up to Bill Bufton's to get the bread.' 'No wonder he couldn't hear me' said Papa, 'I was out on the road ringing the bell.'

'Go back out on the road and ring the bell, Papa,' said Mother. 'He will surely hear it and come back down. I will go and see if Granny is alright. Go with Papa, David.'

So I walked with Papa out on the road in the weak moonlight and bitter cold, tolling the bell to summon Father home. Mother came back up from the cottage saying, 'Hasn't Lew come down yet?'

'No', replied Papa. 'I will go and fetch him,' she said. So hurrying on up the road to Bill Bufton's house she trudged through the snow.

Papa gave up ringing the bell and went to get the ladder out of the shop to rear it up to the chimney so that he could empty a bucket of snow down onto the fire. Mother meanwhile burst into Bill Bufton's house, saying to Father, 'Come down quick, the chimney is on fire at the cottage.'

Father, taking it all very coolly, said 'Alright' and finished his conversation with Bill, while Mother, without stopping hurried back out and down to the cottage. Father duly took his leave and made his way along, taking his time walking down the lane. Mother arrived back at the cottage just in time to try to persuade Papa not to climb up the ladder to the top of the chimney with his bucket of snow. But Papa picked up the bucket and made his way perilously up the ladder, swaying and staggering up into the night towards the flames, while Mother was at the foot of the ladder frightened to death that at any moment he would fall, blind and old as he was. Arriving at the top of the chimney he turned the bucket upside down into the inferno. Out fell only a little bit of snow. The bucket remained over three-quarters full, the contents frozen solid, and no amount of banging the bucket on top of the chimney would dislodge it.

Father arrived on the scene, saying, 'Awh, let the old place burn down and we will build a new one,' followed by 'Oh well, we will have to get the force pump on this job.' So he went up to the shop and brought the force pump down, setting it up in a tin bath outside the back door with a hosepipe running into the living-room

My father at the time of the First World War.

fireplace. While Father got busy breaking through the stonework with a hammer and cold chisel, the others fell to with buckets to fill the bath from the well, the water-butts being frozen. Having broken through the wall, Father was able to direct the spray from the pump onto the inside of the beam where it was burning. I can picture them all now, with the snow lying hard, cold and cruel underfoot, everything cold and frozen. All of them were working hard at it to put the fire out. My sister was holding the lamp to light operations, as it was in the dark shadow round the back of the house. Granny was carrying a small bucket of water from the well to the bath with entreaties from Mother not to overdo it.

Eventually the fire was put out. The beam was burned and charred pretty badly, in fact there wasn't a great deal left of it and Father could push his fist through the holes. The chimney-breast had become too hot to put your hand on, and in the bedroom upstairs there was a black silhouette of a picture of Papa that had been hanging on the chimney wall. The wall had become so hot that it singed the string that was holding the picture on the wall-hook and broke it. The back of the picture was all brown and charred. In fact the resounding thump of the picture hitting the bedroom floor upstairs had been the first clue that something was amiss. Papa and Granny had to sleep up at the bungalow with us that night and for many nights to follow, until Father could carry out repairs.

While Papa and Granny were staying with us after the fire, one afternoon the wind got up and there followed the greatest storm of wind I've ever known. I believe it was a Sunday night, as Father had set out for Wednesbury and became marooned at Pembridge by trees across the road. The wind was howling and roaring, and whistling in the chimney, the strongest blasts making the bungalow shudder. Papa said from the sofa, 'If this wind gets much stronger, we will be out on the road before long.'

Mother said 'Alright, then we will have to go up to Holborn, that's a good strong house up there.' Holborn farm was just up the lane from us. Eventually we all retired to bed, with much calling back and forth to enquire if everybody was alright.

Next morning the storm had blown itself out, and Mother and I made our way up the lane to Holborn for the milk. Arriving in the yard we looked in amazement at the good strong house that Mother had talked of sheltering in last night. The back kitchen was in ruins. The kitchen chimney had blown over and crashed down through the roof. Mrs. Lloyd, telling us about it afterwards, said they had just moved out of the back kitchen into the adjoining room when there was a violent gust of wind which shook the sash windows alarmingly, followed by a terrific crash as the chimney came down through the roof. The wind coming through the adjoining door blew the light out, leaving them all in darkness. They did not know what had happened and it was some time before they could find out, as they had to grope around in the darkness to find the matches before they could get a light. By a dint of good fortune, they had moved to the other room just in time.

There's one thing I must explain about myself in amongst these stories of my family, and that is my deafness. What seems odd now is that none of us realised at first that I was becoming deaf. However, it was brought home to me very forcefully one day when I must have been between 8 and 11 years old and was going to go rabbiting with my dog Ieun. Ieun was a cross between a fox terrier and a collie who had needed a new home and had been brought back by my father one day to replace my previous dog Smut. Smut had been killed in a freak accident, having been hit in the head by a stone shot up from under the wheel of a passing car. Ieun and I both enjoyed our rabbiting, and this would have been during the Second World War when rabbits were a great source of food. So, on this one day, Mother, Father and I were stood by the back door and as Father moved away into the house I said to Mother, 'I'm going rabbiting, come on Ieun.' Without more ado we were away, running across the plock and through a hole in the hedge before Mother could say 'Jack Robinson', or so I thought.

Some hours later we returned empty-handed, muddy and weary. On going into the house to look for Father and not finding him, I asked Mother where he was.

'Well, he's gone back to work,' she said.

'Why didn't you tell me that he was going?' I asked, for I'd wanted to go with him to the sawmill near Rhayader where he was then working and spend the week there with him in the cabin.

'David,' said Mother looking at me intently, 'when you ran off across the plock I shouted and shouted to you to come back so we could tell you he was going and you never answered. I'm sure you can't hear.'

I wasn't having that. At my age deafness was for old people like Grandad, but not me. 'Of course I can hear, Mother. I can hear, I can hear everything.'

Come the following Friday evening, Father arrived home from the sawmill and we all sat around the table having our tea. For the life of me I could not catch every word that he was saying. I kept asking him to repeat it. In exasperation he said, 'Oh, go down to the doctor and get your ears syringed out, you can't hear what I'm saying. Your ears are all blocked up. What you want is one of those old curlews to shove his beak in through one ear and out through the other.'

Somewhat dismayed at being told for the second time in a few days that I could not hear, I replied with some heat, 'I'm not going down to the old doctor. No, I'm not going.'

However, parental force proved stronger and I was duly taken down to the doctor's surgery in Eardisley, and so began a series of visits to consultants in Hereford and later in Worcester. These visits seemed interminable, with a variety of tests being conducted with no obvious results, to me at least, until I was examined by this one particular doctor. Maybe he was a bit smarter than the others. Having sat me down opposite him, he asked, 'Can you hear what I am saying, David?'

'Yes,' I replied.

'You can hear everything I am saying?'

'I can hear everything you say,' I replied, with a nod of my head to lend more strength to my words.

Whereupon he picked up a folder off his desk and held it in front of his mouth. His eyes bored into mine. Not a word could I hear. Suddenly and forcefully the silence struck me. Yet I resisted the urge to get up and take the folder away from his mouth so that I could see what he was saying. I was staggered. Only now did I realise that I was deaf and that I had learnt to lip read as my hearing gradually faded. Astounded disappointment welled up larger and larger in my chest. I slumped down in the chair as the doctor put the folder down on the desk and turned to speak to Mother. I do not remember anything else of the interview with that doctor, but it led to my being fitted with a hearing aid.

Going home with Mother on the bus later that day, I never spoke one word all the 25 or so miles except to ask her 'What did the doctor say when he held that folder in front of his mouth?'

She replied, '"What am I saying now, can you hear me now?" Did you hear him ask you that?'

'No', I said with a slow sorrowful shake of my head, and turned to look out through the window at the countryside. But there was no beauty in it now.

Sometime later at Cooper's Cottage, Mother told Granny Price that I was deaf. 'Never mind David, you can see'. I had already thought of that, but not wanting to hear any more of that sort of talk, I let myself out of the house and made my way up the path and leaned on the garden gate. After a while Grandad came to join me, and I turned to look at him. Grandfather was deaf himself through old age. He returned my look and said, 'So, you're deaf, David?'

'Yes.'

'Never mind, it would be a lot worse if you couldn't see,' he said, trying to cheer me up. But I would not be cheered up, and so Grandfather continued talking to me trying to put me in a better frame of mind. Poor old Grandad, he was deaf and nearly blind as well.

For several days afterwards I was in a low frame of mind, getting much comfort in the companionship of Ieun as we roamed the fields. However, I picked up and started to enjoy life again. There was so much to do and see. Life had indeed become wonderful once more and the beauty of the countryside took on a new meaning for me.

From an early age Father and Grandfather had always treated me as an adult by including me in their work, telling me what they were doing, explaining to me the reasons, the hows and whyfores of how to do certain jobs. I knew the functions of various parts of steam and oil engines and how to repair and mend them, and

Learning the rudiments of mechanics watched by Granny Price.

also the various forms of joinery and how to make them. Father and Grandfather now seemed to redouble their efforts. I would watch for ages any job that they were doing, asking innumerable questions and having it explained to me in very graphic terms so that I could understand what every part did.

Eventually I was fitted up with a hearing aid. This cost Father 20 guineas, a lot of money in those days. But it didn't put things right. I thought I would be able to hear once again, but it was not to be. The last thing I ever heard properly was, 'This is the BBC Home Service, here is the News. British troops are advancing in France and Flanders.' At least, that's what it sounded like to me, though whether I recall this quite right I'm not now sure, but it must have been sometime after D-Day.

The hearing aid had valves in it and would not stand too much rough handling, which often happened and so it would be out of use for a while. This led to many problems at school. One day, when not wearing it as it wasn't working, I couldn't hear the teacher, and when I said 'Pardon', I could see the rage well up in his face as he shouted at me 'Where is your wireless?' (The term hearing aid was rarely used in those days.)

'It's broken, so I left it in my desk in the other classroom.'

'Well, go and get it', he said, shouting all the more and advancing on me like a raging bull, catching my collar and yanking me roughly up out of the desk. Still holding my collar he marched me through the classroom and out through the door, before proceeding to beat me about the head mercilessly. His arms going like windmills, he rained heavy blows down upon me. By now I was bent over double, walking slowly backwards with my arms raised above my head trying to ward off the blows. For twenty yards I staggered backwards, gradually sinking towards the ground and worrying about falling over and cracking my head on some concrete steps that I knew were behind me. Out of the corner of my eye I caught sight of a bosom pal of mine with a look of horror on his face as he stared out of the classroom window. Suddenly the blows ceased and abruptly turning from me without a word, the teacher made his way back to the classroom.

Feeling badly shaken mentally and physically, and with my head ringing, I leaned on the low brick wall by the steps. This was the only time I felt like giving up, but school days in general were definitely not the best time of my life. One teacher once said to me (and he was only one of many), 'There is very little or no hope at all for you.' If ever I needed a put down, this was it. Thank God that I did not believe him and that I had a mind of my own. Not one word did I say to my parents about how I was treated, except to ask on certain days if I could stop at home, but 'No' was the answer every time.

Eventually I left this school and went to one for the partially deaf where I got on very well with the teachers. However, I feel I learnt more later from my time with Papa Price and Father in the days when the age of steam were coming to an end. I was always an eager pupil and helper of theirs, but when young might tire.

At one time Papa Price used to have a very old oil engine driving an overhead shaft in the blacksmith's shop. Belted up to this shaft was the lath and drill. However, someone forgot to let the water out of the oil engine and one night of a very sharp frost the water froze and burst the engine very badly. It happened when they were all working away from home, threshing at a farm where they would sleep. There used to be no coming home at nights to sleep in those days, let alone popping home to check up on things unless you were threshing close at hand, but even this would mean a walk home of two or three miles unless they used their push bike, motor-bike or car.

No means of power had been fitted up since the frost burst the oil engine by the time that Papa Price wanted to do some turning in a hurry. So he bored a hole in the post which was holding up the roof of the shed, the post being in the middle of the building, put a shaft through the hole, fitted a handle and pulley on one end and ran a belt up to the pulley on the lath at the other. Then he came up to the bungalow to see Mother about collaring me as the source of power. Mother said to me 'Papa wants you to help him, go along with him.'

Running on ahead of him down the path I was very proud of myself that I was going to help him to do some real men's work. I was 5 or 6 years old at the time.

Arriving in the shop Papa showed me the handle, took me over to the lath and explained to me what he was going to do and what he wanted me to do. Papa took up his position by the lath while I grasped the handle with my small hands. So with a nod and word from Papa off we went, with myself turning away at the handle for all I was worth. Papa shouted at me 'Not so fast boy, not so fast.'

After what seemed a long time, which must have been only twenty minutes to half an hour, I was slowing down pretty badly and swapping arms as the one arm got tired. Papa was now shouting 'Faster boy, faster boy.' Eventually I ran out of steam and stopped. I could go no more. Papa looking round at me said 'What's the matter boy?'

'I want a rest,' I said.

'Oh dear,' he said. 'Sit down a bit then.'

So there was Papa and myself both sat down in the shop, myself resting and Papa waiting for me to regain some strength. As much as I wanted to keep going, I just could not do so. I was most annoyed and ashamed of myself that I did not have the strength to keep up this endless turning.

This went on all morning with bouts of turning and resting. After a stop for dinner it was off to go again with a will. After a long spell of this I got bored with just turning the handle. So, much to Papa's annoyance, I kept stopping and going to have a look at what he was doing. After telling me once more what he was turning and how it all worked, I wanted him to turn the handle so I could have a go on the lath. 'No, no, no, boy you can't do it. You're not tall enough to reach the travel.'

'I will stand on a bench,' I ventured. 'No, no,' said Papa, shaking his head. I could see that this was not going to be allowed at any cost and no amount of arguing on my part was going to be of any avail. By this time, as the afternoon advanced, I was getting heartily sick of all this turning of the handle. Come the next time I was due for a rest, I bolted. Before Papa could turn round I was gone. So there I was hiding all round the shop inside and outside with Papa looking for me and finding me sometimes and persuading me to do some more turning for him. He was very annoyed with me, but never once did he use force or lay a hand on me. After yet another spell of turning I bolted out of the shop up the path and into the bungalow, not saying a word to Mother as I sat down in the armchair for a well earned rest. After a while Papa came to the door and Mother said once more, 'Go and help Papa, David.'

I went halfway down the path with him and bolted again. I just could not face any more of this boring turning. I made sure of a good hiding place and from it I could see poor old Papa wandering round looking for me. After a long spell of time had elapsed I decided to go and offer my services again.

Well, to cut a long story short, this put me off any kind of hand power turning for life. I also hated the hand pumping of water in order to fill a tank, for that's another boring job. I am not talking about pumping for half an hour, but all day for two or three days.

Father once told me how he had to turn the handle for the lath for four days non stop from early in the morning until it was too dark to see to do any more work at night. This was for the Old Man at Pentrejack. How he could stick that, I shall never know.

Gwyn, the Old Man's son by his second wife, and Lucy were the last of the Price family to live at Pentrejack, returning to live there at the end of the First World War after the Old Man had died. One day a message came up from them – would I go down and help to move Gwyn's supply of winter coal out of the yard, where it had been unloaded, into the back kitchen cum coal store? So taking myself off down the road to Pentrejack one Saturday morning, I presented myself to Gwyn all ready to start work to move nigh on 2 tons of coal. I had to shovel the coal into a wheelbarrow and then wheel it through the main living room, entering by the front door. The living room also served as the kitchen where all the cooking and eating of meals took place. The back kitchen served as a place to wash your hands in a bowl of water which was resting on a table, also for keeping the buckets of water used for household purposes (the water being obtained from the pump over the well just outside the front door) and for storing the coal. The door to the back kitchen was on the far side of the living room.

The barrow was an old wooden one with a wooden wheel and an iron tyre that made a good rumbling noise as you wheeled it along, juddering and thumping over the cobbles outside, the juddering shocks travelling up your arms from the handles. As I went through the door into the back kitchen, just missing the grandfather clock, I was told more than once 'You mind that clock, that's George's clock.' The Old Man bought it at Kington in 1865 for £4 10s.

It was a slow job, as on reaching the back kitchen I had to build a wall of coal with the largest lumps just so far out from the wall and then fill the void that was formed with smaller lumps of coal and slack all neat and tidy like. It was a cold east windy day in the late autumn – too cold to take your jacket off, but too warm to keep it on while you were working. After having moved many barrowloads and getting somewhat warm, I offed with my jacket. 'Ou I, Ou I,' shouted Gwyn his moustache bristling and annoyance showing in every line of his face, 'you put that jacket back on at once boy or you'll catch your death.' 'It's cold,' he said, raising his hand to feel the east wind. (I always had trouble lip reading Gwyn for his moustache effectively covered his upper lip and I can't lip read someone with only one lip showing!)

My uncle, Gwyn Price.

I thought it best to humour him. 'Alright, alright,' I replied, hastily slipping it back on.

Gwyn, realizing why I had taken it off, then said, 'Have a drink of cider, boy.'

'Alright,' I replied, 'I be somewhat thirsty.'

So out of the house comes Gwyn with a great big cup full of cider.

'Thanks,' I said, taking the cup off him as he handed it to me and hurried off back into the house. Strange, I thought to myself as I watched his hastily retreating figure.

Looking forward to quenching my thirst, I rose the cup to my lips and drank long, hard and deep, then grabbed my throat with one hand and nearly passed out. My throat felt as if it had been cut wide open from the inside out. That cider was sharp enough to cut a good sized tree in half. It tasted more like vinegar. Peering into the cup at the amber liquid with a tiny bit of straw floating on it and greatly disappointed with it, I could see that I had drunk less than half of the cup and it was a cup of some size. So, resting it on the side of a threshing drum and keeping a wary eye on it I took a sip now and again. After bowling several more barrowloads of coal into the house and once more tackling the cider, liking it less and less and not lowering the level of it much, I thought to myself 'I can't manage all this.' So, casting my eyes round to make sure Gwyn wasn't about, I emptied it out, breathing a sigh of relief as the last drop disappeared into the ground.

I had just turned the cup the right way up in my hand when around the corner of the drum out of nowhere springs Gwyn. 'Heck,' I thought, 'I hope he never saw me empty the cup.'

Gwyn, noting the empty cup in my hand, said 'Have another cup boy' while peering at me hard from underneath the poke of his cap.

'Noooo thanks,' I said, handing him the cup and at the same time hurriedly shovelling coal into the barrow. But I noticed the twinkle in his eye and the slight smile as he turned away from me to take the cup back into the house.

Come dinner time Gwyn said to me, 'Come on in the house and have a bit of dinner, boy.' So having washed my hands in the back kitchen in the bowl of soapy water and sat down at the table ready to start dinner, I was waiting for Gwyn who was bent over the fire making the tea. Gwyn and Lucy were now very old and frail and Gwyn was getting the dinner as Lucy could not now do too much. Gwyn's hands were shaking like a leaf as he poured the tea. With the teapot wagging about he aimed the spout at the cups and spilled some tea onto the flagstone floor by Lucy's feet. After putting the pot back down on the hob by the fire to keep warm, he turned back to the table, grinning, with his moustache drooping down over his lips, which were all of a quiver.

He said to me, pointing to the spilled tea on the floor by Lucy's feet, 'Her's wet herself.'

'Oh, isn't he awful,' said Lucy, all coy like a young girl.

I was enjoying this little bantering between the old couple, but not knowing what to say I just smiled.

After dinner while Gwyn was putting the food by in the three corner cupboard which was hung on the wall over the deal dinnertable, I went and sat on the settle which was on the opposite side of the fire for a few minutes rest. My eyes strayed upwards to the great chamfered beams in the ceiling and I wondered if these were ever ship timbers from Aberystwyth or if one of the Prices had chamfered them out with the adze years ago.

On the meat cratch (rack) were several muzzle loading guns and a shotgun called Short Jim, as the end of the barrel had been shortened due, I believe, to being damaged. It had been given to the Old Man by Jim Saveker who went to America and was never heard of again. We often wondered what became of him.

That night as we were having tea I mentioned Gwyn's cider to Father saying what terrible stuff it was. Father, much amused, said, 'I know, I had some myself years ago. Gwyn used to make it by mashing a few apples up in the bottom of a barrel.'

'Gosh,' I said, 'that's why the straw was in it and I could not even get my breath.'

'Yes,' he replied, 'it makes good vinegar and we very often used it as such.'

A few years later I was up at Ty-Bach at Llowes with Maurice, Gwyn's brother, when he enquired off me if I would like a glass of cider.

'Nooo, not just now thanks, I'll have a drop another time,' I replied, edging towards the car. 'I'd better be getting along Maurice.'

Maurice nodded his head slightly as if to say, 'Ah well, next time.'

Going down the pitch in the car from Ty-Bach, 'Cor,' I thought to myself, 'that was close! I must be ready for it next time. I don't fancy any more of that stuff.'

2 Father's First World War Memories

Sometimes while we were sat by the old cooking range, with the lamp casting its hushed yellow glow about the room and the dance of the firelight making it hard for me to lip read in the shadows, Father related his experiences in France during the First World War. Some of the stories were sad, some amusing, some strange, some of sights that he had witnessed which were too horrible to recall to mind or now to put on paper. I hoped and prayed that I should never be called to fight in any war.

After tea one night I asked Father 'How did it come about that you joined the army and went to war?'

'Oh, I volunteered,' he replied looking at me and holding my eye. 'I felt it was my duty to go. I joined up with H.G. We went up to Shrewsbury together, getting on the train at Hereford station. We made an agreement that we would stick together through thick and thin, whatever happened. At this particular time H.G. was suffering from a very bad cold and he was extremely poorly indeed. The cold had also made him temporarily deaf, and while we were waiting in the queue to be examined, he fainted. He was one ahead of me in the queue and went in before me and I think he played on this cold of his. Later he approached me and said, "You know, I think I've got a chance of getting out of the army." He did, and he got away with it. So I was left alone,' said Father pursing his lips. The look on his face said it all.

'What a friend!' I said.

'He told me later, after his examination, that as he was leaving the room they said to him, "Shut the door", but he didn't stop,' said Father.

'Did he hear them?' I asked.

'Oh yes, he told me he heard them alright. "But I didn't stop, I kept going," he said.'

'So old H.G. never went out to France?' I asked.

'No,' replied Father, shaking his head.

'He never fought in the war at all?'

Father continued shaking his head.

'Well, well,' I said, 'he wasn't much of a friend. Did you see him or meet him much after the war?'

'Oh yes,' replied Father. 'Before the war we used to see quite a lot of one another, but not so much after.'

'No, I can understand that,' I said.

The seriousness on Father's face lightened and turned to laughter. 'After the war old H.G. got hold of some medals from somewhere and was walking down the street in Kington with these medals pinned to his chest. The policeman who was there at that time knew H.G. and knew that he had not served in the war, so approached him and made him take them off.'

I dwelt on what Father had been saying for a few minutes, and as the silence lengthened between us I looked at my boots steaming on the fender. I said, 'These old boots of mine are heavy.'

'Heavy?' said Father, looking at me. 'No, no, those old boots that I used to wear in the army were far heavier than those,' nodding towards my boots.

My father in his KSLI uniform

'I know,' I said. 'I tried wearing them for a spell. It was like having two anvils on my feet until I got used to them.'

'Yes, they were very heavy,' he replied. 'When I was out in France I had a terrible carbuncle on my foot and it became a great hole,' he said, grimacing at the memory of it. 'I had been suffering with it a lot for some time. However after a lot of bother I had managed to obtain a pair of boots that were fairly comfortable, in particular the one for my bad foot. But this carbuncle was still playing me up something terrible and I could hardly put my foot to the ground. When I went to the army doctor he would lance it, but this was no good. It was far better to let it come to a head and burst.

'One day I was taken ill and was carried into hospital on a stretcher. When I got better I was told to go through a doorway which they pointed out to me, get my boots and rejoin my Company. Walking through the doorway I expected to find my own boots, but facing me was the biggest pile of boots I had ever seen. They would have filled this room up easy. They reached right up to the ceiling, all of them chucked in a heap, rights and lefts any old how. So my well fitted boot that I went to so much trouble to obtain for my bad foot was gone. Well, I searched for another good boot for my bad foot, and eventually I found one, but it was nothing like as good or as comfortable a fit as the one I lost. So nursing my foot I set out to rejoin my Company. When I got to where they had been, they had moved and I had to make some enquiries to find out their whereabouts, which turned out to be twenty or thirty miles away. I had a lift in a lorry, but he only took me a very small part of the way and it was a day or two before I finally found them.

'It was night-time when I arrived and discovered that I had not got my blanket. What became of it I don't know. I never had it when I came out of hospital. So I had one of those fellows who had come up through the ranks berating me for losing my blanket; these fellows were very often the worst. However, an officer came along who in civilian life was gentry. He said, "Don't worry about your blanket, I'll find you a blanket," and he did.

'In one of the bell-tents that we used to sleep in, some of our food kept being taken. How, who or what was taking it we hadn't the foggiest idea. We never saw anybody take it, although we kept watch. We hung it on the tent pole in the middle of the tent with some coats, to be out of reach of any rats, but still it went missing. There wouldn't be any crumbs on the floor or any sign of food about anywhere. It was a mystery how it was being taken.

'However, I was in the tent resting my foot, all very quiet, when I noticed a movement right up at the top of the tent where it folded over the pole. It was a rat. Down the tent pole creeps the rat and I watched him take some food, crawl back up the pole to the top and disappear into the folds of the tent. So that's how he did it, the crafty thing. Later we fetched him down.'

Mother looked up from her reading, saying, 'You didn't eat that food after the rat had been in there, did you?'

Father looked at me and burst out laughing. 'Eat it? Of course we ate it, there was nothing else.'

Mother pulled a face, saying 'That's horrible.'

He turned to me one evening saying how moved he was when arriving home on leave unexpectedly, he lifted the latch on the door and entered the dear old cottage to find no one about. But the table had been laid for tea with the most beautiful pristine white tablecloth and the crocks all glowing white. 'I stood and gazed at it for some minutes, and oh, the cleanness and the whiteness of it! After living in the mud and filth out in France, it was a sight that I had forgotten. I had clean forgot that anything could be so clean and white. The emotion welled up in me, tears clouded my eyes. It was a sight and a moment that I shall never forget.'

I tried to capture the thoughts in a poem:

Beyond the thunder of the guns
Beyond this quaking land
Beyond the treacherous sea
Lies England.
Place of sublime peace and safety
Which I long once more to see
And on dear old Brilley Mountain
Down the little mountain lane
Just beyond the pool
In the cleft upon the bank
Rests the old by tack [a local name for the cottage]
And beneath the stone tiled roof
Lies our humble cottage that I call home.

Among this mud and slime
Among this land of death and strife
A vision of the dear old cottage
Appears before mine eyes
And beneath the shadows of the beams
The tablecloth in all its prismatic glory
Adecked with crocks all glowing white.

On another evening Father told me, 'When we were marching along, going towards the Front, I was intrigued by a number of heaps that we passed. These heaps were by the roadside, covered with tarpaulins, ever so many of them, spaced out at intervals. You couldn't see what was under the tarpaulins. If I had the opportunity I would have gone and found out, but it was not possible to fall out. We had to keep marching. Eventually, as we got nearer the Front, I found out what these heaps were as there was no tarpaulin over them. They were dead bodies, all piled up.'

One of the things that I recall him saying was how the ground would be all of a tremble from the big guns firing as they shelled the enemy lines. Father heaved a sigh and shook his head at the memory of it all. I gazed into the fire and thought about his stories, the thunder and rumbling of the guns that set the earth a-trembling, and the strange and terrific destruction that explosives did. The howl of the shells, the trenches, the foot step, the mud and the shell holes. The enemy snipers and how they achieved a hit. The young lads who put their ages up to get in the war, of whom Uncle Tom (my mother's brother) was one and had both his legs machine-gunned off. The names and places he had seen and been to. The landscape, the state of the country, the houses, the people and some of their ways. And the awful and terrible things that war did, which are best left unsaid.

The thoughts of the unfruitfulness of war kept our minds occupied for a few moments. Then a movement from Father arrested my attention. I turned to face him as he started to speak to me.

'At one time out in France,' he said, 'we could see a wood in the distance. Night was falling and we had made up our minds that this wood was going to be our shelter for the night. It wasn't much of a wood really, just a small coppice, but we were dog tired and so we bedded down for the night. We were that tired, we slept like logs all the night long. Yes, we were absolutely clean worn out.

'On getting up next morning, going to the edge of the wood and looking out, we stopped dead, our eyes popping out. We could not believe the sight that was before us. There lined up facing us was a row of guns.' Father paused, looking at me.

'Gosh, Germans,' I said.

'They had come in during the night and we never heard a thing. Not a sound, not a jingle did we hear. Lucky for us that they were our own guns. If they had been German guns we wouldn't have had a chance,' he said, shaking his head.

'Another time and place we were all bedded down for the night out in the open. It was a cold, frosty night, with a clear moonlight lighting up the landscape. We had more or less got off to sleep when an officer came round waking us up. He was all hot and bothered and made us take our blankets or ground sheets off. He reckoned that any enemy aircraft flying overhead would see the frost reflecting on our blankets in the moonlight and identify us. So we had no covering that night.'

'And you slept like that all night?' I asked.

'Yes,' he said.

'Do you think that the Germans could have seen you from their aircraft flying overhead?'

Father lifted his eyebrows and shoulders at the same time saying 'I don't know.'

'When the war was over we had our orders. "Get your boots repaired and go and bury the dead." Well, I was two or

A card of the King's Shropshire Light Infantry, in which Father served in the First World War.

three days in the queue waiting to get my boots repaired, by which time the dead were more or less buried. But we had to go and bury the horses then.'

'Heck,' I said, 'that was an awful job.'

'Yes,' he replied, 'but it was a lot better than burying the dead.'

'You would have to dig a big hole to bury horses,' I ventured.

'Yes, not only that but the horses were rotten and swelled up and when you caught hold of one of them by the leg to pull it into a hole, the leg came off.'

When the war was over my father said that the Chinese and Japanese who had fought with the Allies fell out and started fighting. Father and his Company had orders to arm up and get between them to restore order, but they were warned time and again not to shoot. They hurried off to the trouble spot only to find that all was quiet and there was not a sound or a soul about. The Chinese, on seeing the Japs coming for them, had took to their heels and fled, apparently only stopping once they reached a place some 40 miles away. He said the Chinese used to like making tea and flying kites in camp.

It wasn't only around the fire in the evening that Father would tell me stories of the war. Sometimes memories would come back when we were at work. One cold, wet, miserable winter's day, we were digging a trench to receive one-inch galvanized iron pipes for a water supply system taking water to various drinking tanks round the farm on which we were working. We had already built the pump house down by the well and the reservoir up on the hill. All told there was several hundred yards of trenching and piping to be carried out with the necessary thread cutting, fitting and connections to be made. The trench itself was to be two foot six inches deep at five shillings a yard, including pipe laying and fitting, also back filling of the earth into the trench.

All morning the cold wind and rain had been knifing through us, with the drizzle lying damp on our shoulders, seeping through our old long macks and mingling with the sweat of our labours as it trickled down our backs. We felt cold, wet and starved whenever we paused for a rest. The damp and muddy macks were awkward and restricted our movements, whilst the rain wetted the handles of our pick-axes and shovels, making them cold, unpleasant and slippery to the grasp, with the mud sticking heavy and cumbersome to our boots. It was an altogether uncomfortable working day as we raised and let fall our pick-axes, then shovelled out the spoil onto the uphill side of the trench (making it easier to push back in), as we steadily advanced yard by yard across the field.

Come dinner time we stacked our picks in the lee of the trench and made our way down to the old barn below us to have some respite from the elements while we partook of our meal, taking our shovels with us in order to keep the handles as dry as possible, as it is most unpleasant working all day long with sopping wet handles.

Entering the barn, which was open on one side, fortunately for us the open side being in the lee of the wind, I sank wearily down onto the straw and hay, and stretched out full length, only too glad of a rest before starting on my sandwiches, while the musty smell from the straw rose around me to be quickly dispersed by the draught.

Thinking of all the digging ahead of us, I rolled over onto my side and looking at Father I said, 'Could you manage the Roby and a mole plough in these fields?'

'No, no it would be no good,' he answered. 'We would be bogged down in no time,' rapidly shaking his head at the thought of it, as it was the middle of winter and the ground in many places was waterlogged.

'Brrrr, it's cold in here,' I said, casting a look behind me hoping that I could see where the draught was coming from, so that I could stuff some straw into the hole. But seeing no likely looking place, I struggled down into the straw, saying, 'I hope it's a bit warmer tomorrow.'

'Yes,' said Father. Then with hardly a pause he added, 'No, no this is a real good place,' peering up at the roof and looking round the building. 'If we could have found a place like this out in France during the war it would have been untold luxury.' Still looking round, 'Yes', he said, 'a barn as good as this would have been a wonderful place. I can remember at one time we went into an old barn to find a bit of shelter. However, inside this barn it was a job to find a dry place as the rain was pouring in everywhere. I was not feeling too good, so I lay down on what appeared to be a heap of corrugated iron. This was just a little distance from the other men who were sat down together. As I lay there I started to shiver, but I got off to sleep and unknown to me I shuddered violently all night long. In fact so violent was my shivering that I started the iron under me rattling like the clappers and the other men could not sleep for the racket that I was making. They told me next day that the din was something awful and they swore that I was dying and they did not expect to see me alive in the morning.'

'Whatever was the matter with you?' I asked.

'I don't know', he replied. 'But I was alright next morning and I slept alright throughout the night.'

'Did you know that you were shivering like that, and did you ever have it again?'

'No,' he replied to both questions, shaking his head, then starting his sandwiches.

'Oh well, I suppose the old barn isn't too bad after all,' I said. 'No doubt it was a lot worse out in France with death staring you in the face all the time.'

Father looked at me and said not a word, only giving a slight nod with his head and continuing to eat his sandwiches.

I got down deeper into the straw, trying to get some warmth and shelter from the draught, poured myself a cup of tea and opened my bate box. And so the silence of my deaf world enfolded itself around us as I gazed out at the fog and the water droplets dropping from the eaves.

In a while we both heaved a sigh and quietly shut our bate boxes, screwed the cups back on our now empty flasks, put them in our bags and climbed stiffly to our feet, picked up our shovels and made our way back up the field through the rain and fog to our place of work. Climbing down into the muddy trench and grasping the pick, I peered through glooming rain up the line of the trench, past Father who was working some fifteen to twenty yards ahead of me. I could see no Angels of Mons to lighten the gloom. Looking backwards behind me down the length of the trench, I was thankful that there was no enemy at my heels and that I was not out in a trench in France. Turning back to my work, I raise the pick above my head and bring it down, driving the point into the good earth, and lever out the spoil. There will be a few more hours of digging and then we will have to get the pipes in before the night falls.

I notice that Father has paused and is listening intently. I stop too and look around to see if I can see what he can hear, at the same time striving to hear with what limited hearing I've got. Some soil trickles down onto my foot. 'Can you hear gunfire, Father?' I ask.

'No, we're not out in France,' he replies, with an almost invisible smile and quick, small shake of his head. 'It must be the buzzing in my ears.'

And so we continue our work until darkness calls a halt.

One day while talking about the war, when Father was now very much advanced in years, in his nineties, I recall saying to him, 'It would have been far better to have given you soldiers some money than those medals. About fifty pounds would have been more help to you. That would have been a considerable amount in those days.'

'You can have them for fifty if you like,' he replied, laughing.

3 Threshing, Sawing and other work

The Old Man had used the Marshall and various portable engines in his threshing work, and just before the First World War Papa Price bought a Fowler traction engine that had been built in 1908 and came with the name Nil Desperandum on the boiler. Literally meaning 'Never Despair', Nil Desperandum was to become my personal motto. Papa had to collect the engine from the other side of Raglan, a journey of fifty or sixty miles, and it took him and Father all day. They shut off steam and dropped the damper in the yard at Pentrejack at nine o'clock that night. 'My word I was tired,' said Father. 'I was glad to climb down from the engine.'

The Old Man walked round the Fowler with the lantern, comparing it with the old Marshall of the 1800s, shaking his head ponderously before delivering his verdict: 'It's too complicated.' The Marshall was a steam-driven ploughing machine which he had bought from a farm in Lyonshall, and was very much the Old Man's engine. He also used it for threshing. In those days self-propelled engines had to be registered in each county in which they travelled, and the Marshall was the twenty-third such engine registered in Herefordshire, and the very first in Radnorshire.

Father told me one story of when the Old Man, Papa Price, he and his brother Idris were on their way to thresh at the little Gaer Farm just off the Common on Brilley Mountain one year shortly before the First World War. They were climbing Tiddly-wink bank with the old Marshall. (There used to be a man living at Caebedw Cottage, at one time known as The

Papa Price's old Fowler, Nil Desperandum. Built in 1908, no.11595, it was a single cylinder 7 horsepower engine. Grandfather's worker Old Tom is stood by the wheel.

Four Winds, which is at the top of the bank, and he had a daughter whom some boys used to come to visit. He was highly displeased with this state of affairs and ordered the boys off, saying 'I'm not having any boys coming tiddly-winking around the girl.' And that's how the house became known locally as Tiddly-wink.)

'The old Marshall was putting her back into it, pulling the portable and the drum behind her, bellowing up the chimney, shooting the sparks high into the night sky. Nearing the crest of the bank just below Caebedw Cottage, the back wheels started to fly round, losing their grip and cutting the road up, bringing the tack to a stop. The old Marshall hove to with a work-worn weary sigh from years of toil as Papa Price shut off. It was pitch dark and we could hardly see what we were doing. Also it was getting late. So we decided to leave the tack by the side of the road for the night. With the aid of a bit of light from the lantern we eased the portable and drum on to the side of the road, leaving just enough room for a horse and trap to squeeze by. Papa Price then drove the engine on up the bank, drawing off the road by Caebedw Cottage, where we left it overnight. We all took ourselves off home to bed, the Old Man, then in his seventies, walking back down to Pentrejack.

'Come next morning we decided to take a load of stone off the Common over to the engine to put under the wheels and fill the holes in the road that we had made. One of us went to light a fire in the engine and the others went over to the Gaer to borrow the horse and gambo [cart].'

The Roby and the Fowler in the yard at Perryn. When grandfather died, I was missing him sorely. The shop was now a sad and lonely place so I climbed up on the Fowler and once again I imagined I was with him firing up the engine, working the injector and pump, breaking coal in the bunker, opening the regulator to give her a bit more, winding the brake on and hauling back on the reverse lever, as we thundered down Penlan Pitch, heading out for the Great Beyond.

At this point, Uncle took over the story, as it was he that went to the Gaer. Returning with the horse and gambo, they gathered some stone which lay along the roadside and returned to where the tack was stood. 'When we got to the tack, we put some stone down and got the tack up the bank and over the crest onto the bit of flat. Now all coupled up and ready to get on, we walked back down the road to tidy up the damage we had made, filling in the holes and levelling it off. What stone was left over we put in a tidy heap by the side of the road.

'We were reported for stealing stone off the council, but someone higher up said it was not so: "The men were bound to do something to get off the road. As for the stone, it was only taking it from one place and putting it in another place, and you'd better be careful what you say." No more was ever heard about it.'

At one farm where the Old Man used to thresh, he used to put the drum in the barn which was by the side of the road. Having fixed the drum up, he then put the portable the other side of the road and fitted the driving belt up between them. The belt itself was across the road. Every time a horse and trap came along or any of the day's traffic, the engine was shut off, the belt removed, the horse and trap led by, the belt put back on, then the regulator would be opened and off again. Well, this went on for some time and of course the inevitable happened – somebody reported him.

Out came the powers that be and stopped him threshing in this manner, saying 'You're not allowed to do this.' So some other way had to be found to belt the engine up to the drum. No doubt this made it very awkward and a lot more work in fixing the tack up.

Another time, he actually threshed on the road itself. That took place just down below Pentrejack, where a little prill runs under the road. In those days the road was in an extremely rough condition and you had to ford the prill, which was just an open ditch across the road. So rough was the road that they rarely ventured down it with the old Marshall and the tack as it would knock it all about too much. Within a few yards of this prill the Old Man would set up his threshing drum and engine on the road to thresh. The prill was a good source of water. The rick which was to be threshed was in the adjacent field, but the gateway into to it was narrow and the field soft underfoot, so that if they could have even got into the field they would no doubt have been bogged down in the first yard. As it was, the rick was on the other side of the hedge from the road and it was very handy to toss the sheaves over the hedge onto the drum. Any traffic that could not get by had to go through the field gate, pass up the field and go out through a gate at the top.

The old Fowler was to work in Brilley and the surrounding areas for over thirty years at threshing, sawing timber, hauling lime and stone-hauling, and became a well-known engine to all and sundry, serving them faithfully to the end. But it was hard work, for threshing was carried on throughout the winter, the engine often being stationed at a farm for several days. Sometimes Papa Price and Father would stay at the farm where they were working, but at others they would walk from home to work and back each day. When staying at the farm where they were working, Father would want to go to bed early, but the farmers would like to keep him up asking questions about the threshing machines and steam engines. He liked all the folk for whom he threshed and always spoke highly of them, saying how they made him one of them, making him feel very much at home. But when working at farms that were thought to be within commuting range of home, they would get up early on a cold dark winter's morning and walk the miles from Brilley to get steam up in the engine, ready for a day's threshing, followed by the same walk back at night. It would be dark and cold in the winter, very often with an icy east wind cutting into you, and the distance could be 8 or 9 miles, as over the hills to Kitchen Farm at Radnor.

Father told me that sometimes he and Papa Price would share a bicycle to get to and from work. 'After we had settled the tack for the night, Papa Price would start off home on the bike and I would start walking. Papa Price of course soon left me behind. After he had gone a reasonable distance, he got off the bike, left it in the hedge and walked on. Eventually I come along and mounts the bike and start pedalling for home. I eventually caught Papa Price up and passed him, leaving him behind. When I thought I had gone the same distance, I jumps off the bike puts the bike in the hedge and walks on. Along comes Papa, mounts the bike and pedals for home, just now passing me. By repeating this process over and over again, we not only got home quite quickly but also kept warm and sometimes, but not always, arrived in the yard together.'

So, from late summer and through the winter the threshing tack would go from farm to farm. Father was always accompanied by his dog, who was a very good ratter, and when he was moving the tack between farms the dog would make the journey by walking underneath the threshing drum which was pulled behind the engine. Very often, according to the course of the road, with its dips and rises and going round corners, looking back you could only see the dog's four legs rapidly scissoring backwards and forwards as he hurriedly kept pace with the tack.

On one farm where Papa Price worked there was a dog that was good at climbing ladders. When Papa Price was

Threshing at Titley Court with the Fowler. Papa Price is stood in the middle wearing a dark jacket and engineer's cap.

The Fowler Nil Desperandum threshing at a Huntington farm shortly before the outbreak of the First World War. Father is standing on the footplate, Papa Price is by the hind wheel. The man standing between the engine and the drum by the sack lifter is thought to be Mr. Morris of the Little Gaer, and the elderly gentleman stood just in front of the straw tyer is his father. It was not until 1950 that Father showed me these photos, and by that time he couldn't remember who some of the men were. Papa Price had bought the Fowler for £200 and when war broke out he was offered £1,000 to sell it, but turned the offer down.

hard at it separating the seed from the chaff, the pitchers on the rick would call down to the dog which would oblige by climbing up the ladder onto the top of the drum. Everyone enjoyed the spectacle.

But one day disaster struck. The dog climbed the ladder onto the top of the machine, jumped over the drum cover, landing on the other side safely but with his back legs on the iron sheeting leading into the mouth of the drum. And of course the inevitable happened, he slipped backwards down onto the revolving drum, the beaters shredding his hind quarters, stopping the drum, throwing the belt off the pulley, killing him instantly. It was indeed a sad loss, with everybody being most upset as they were all very fond of this dog. It also meant three days of lost threshing while Papa Price removed the drum from the machine, transported it home to the shop to straighten the bent shaft, repair the beaters, balance it up and fit it back in the machine. But the drum never ran the same again, as there was a slight spring in the spindle which could not be discerned by eye alone, and from that day forward there was always a minute vibration throughout the machine.

At a certain farm where Father used to thresh during the days when every farmer's wife made her own bread in the baking oven, the oven itself, as in most farmhouses, was in the kitchen next to the fireplace. The kitchen also served as a living room. At this farm, after the day's baking was completed, they were in the habit of leaving the oven door open. Father didn't know the reason why. It may have been to help to warm the kitchen, or to cool the oven off before putting some morning wood in to dry. It has been known for morning wood to catch alight from putting it in too hot an oven.

However they used to have a dog that if it got the chance would go and lie down just inside the oven door, the oven being a nice warm place like a centrally heated dog kennel. One evening after the day's baking was completed the dog, as usual, seized the opportunity and quietly stole into the oven and stretched out in utter bliss. Later on that evening the farming folk, getting ready to retire for the night, made the fire safe and pushed the oven door shut having failed to notice the dog and forgetting to check if he was in the oven. Next day the dog was missing and could not be found anywhere. The good folk called, shouted and searched, but all in vain. It was indeed a mystery as to what had become of the dog and they talked and wondered about what could have happened to him. And so the days went by and baking day came round once more. Opening the oven door in preparation for lighting the farmer's wife must have recoiled in horror, as there was the dog lying in the mouth of the oven, dead and very dried out, with the skin drawn tightly to be body.

There used to be a saying years ago when the old baking ovens were in regular use. Having got the oven up to heat and put the bread in, if there was enough room just inside the oven door, the housewife would put in a cake and shut the door. When the bread was baked and ready to come out, the cake had to come out first regardless of whether it was fully cooked or not. Sometimes it was not quite cooked, and that's how the saying came about that anyone who was behaving foolish or had acted simple over something 'must have come out with the cake' (half-baked, as you might now say).

When threshing at farms in the depths of winter, the warmth of the engine was a welcome source of comfort. Some of the farms in the Radnorshire hills hardly saw any sun on the days it chose to shine. On one occasion, Father told me, there was an inch of snow on the ground as he climbed down from the engine when the welcome hour of dinner had arrived, when he could sit down in the warmth of the farmhouse and enjoy some respite from the dust and biting wind, and recharge the inner man with good wholesome food, or so he thought. The farmhands had already gone on ahead towards the house, leaving Father to attend to the fire and water in the engine.

As the farmer and Father walked towards the house, the farmer said to him, 'You see that black mark in the snow coming down the side of the mountain?' The mountain was the other side of the farm, about a quarter of a mile away.

'Yes,' replied Father looking up at the mountain that the farmer was pointing out to him. 'I can see it.'

Father with his threshing tack, Roby engine and drum in a barn above Badlands at Kinnerton Court. Father would often feed the drum and let someone else drive the engine, as this was the warmest place to be and it allowed that person to get warm. This is not the same Roby as shown in other photos. When he bought it he borrowed Maurice Price's big Burrell to tow it home from Ross-on-Wye. Note the little water hand cart on the far right which was often used to fetch water for the engine and which has a sack over it to stop the water sloshing out. Also note the crossed belt: Father always crossed the belt when threshing. The photo was taken sometime after the outbreak of the Second World War, as indicated by the white line on the side of the engine which was a requirement during the war to make it more visible to other road users during the blackout.

'Well,' said the farmer, 'that is the mark that your dinner for today made when we dragged it down the mountain. A sheep died on top of the hill, so we dragged it down to the farm, skinned it, dressed it and now we are going to have it for dinner today.'

'Oh,' said Father, the thought putting him off his dinner somewhat. While they were having their dinner and nobody was looking, Father slipped the meat into his pocket. After dinner, when he got back outside and out of sight of anybody, he offered the meat to the farm dog. After sniffing at it a bit, the dog turned up its nose and walked off.

'Well, well,' I said laughing, 'do you think the sheep was fit to eat, having died like that?'

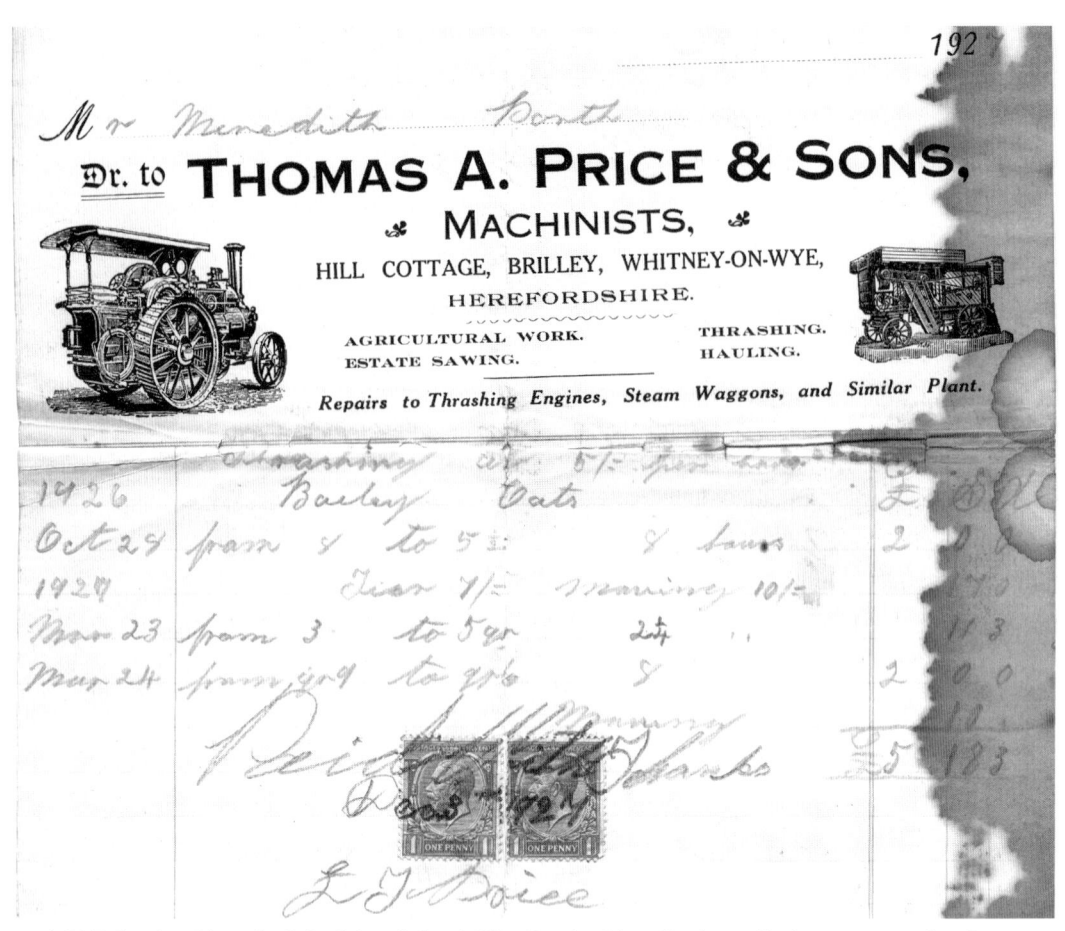

A bill for threshing for Mr. Meredith of The Porth, New Radnor. Father was nearly always paid 12 months in arrears; the 1920s and '30s were very hard times and money was scarce.

'I don't know,' Father replied. 'Everybody went on living, so I don't know why the old dog was so fussy.' We both paused, wondering, as most farm dogs would wolf anything down.

Farmers, or their wives, could certainly be mean. One time when Father was threshing at a farm near Presteigne there was a navvy staying there who was working on the pipeline that carries water from the Elan valley dams to Birmingham. The navvy asked the farm's servant girl if she would clean and blacken his boots, agreeing to pay her a shilling a week. This she did and he duly paid her, whereupon the lady of the house took the money off her, saying that it was hers as she had cleaned the boots in her time and using her boot polish and brushes. So the poor girl never got her money, which would have been a nice sum for her.

At one farm where Father used to thresh, the lady farmer always had to be trying to do several different jobs at once. On this one occasion when Father and Harry had arrived with the tack and made a start on setting it up, they had just missed the normal dinner hour. This meant that it was only Harry and Father who sat down at the table, yet they had only just enough room for their dinner plates – the rest of the table was just loaded up with crocks and all manner of things. The lady farmer was working at the same table doing four different jobs at once: cooking, making bread, feathering and drawing a fowl. She finished drawing the fowl, from which the smell was awful, and without pausing to swill her hands, plunged them straight into a bowl of flour and started kneading it. My father said, 'Having done a bit of that she would turn her hand to something else and so it went on all through our meal. This was a general occurrence during the many times that I had dinner there.'

'At one farm the lady and her daughters were somewhat superior. On showing me where the stairs so I could find my way to bed, the good lady said to me "Sorry we haven't got a back stairs for you to go up, Mr. Price,' to which I replied "That's alright, the front stairs will do."'

Sometimes he would be threshing at one farm, but sleeping at another. On one occasion he and Harry, having finished the day's threshing and had their supper, walked over to the other farm to sleep. When they got there, there wasn't a soul about. Thinking that the farmers must have all gone to bed and with the door only on the latch (nobody locked up in those days) they let themselves in and sat down one each side of the fire, fully expecting someone to come and show them where to sleep. After some time they concluded that everyone really had gone to bed and forgotten about them. So, making up the fire, they settled down for the night. Come four o'clock in the morning they made up the fire again, put the kettle on the sway and set off.

They did not sleep there the next night, having moved on to thresh at another farm. Twelve months later, however, they were back at the farm at which they'd stayed, this time undertaking threshing on site, and talking to the farmer's wife about the night in question she said she could not understand how the fire was in and the kettle boiled when she came into the kitchen next morning, as she was sure she doused the fire for the night. The maid had told her that she saw some shadows cast on the landing by the fire, but was too frightened to make a sound. Father only told them during the next threshing season that he and Harry had stayed the night.

At another farm where he and Harry were sleeping, they had to share the bed, and Father said they couldn't sleep for fleas. 'We were both slapping and scratching, twisting and turning all the night long. They were biting like anything. We were catching them and putting them in the candle. They would go pop. Not able to stick it any longer, we were up before four o'clock in the morning and off out to get steam up.' When people had fleas in those days, you've got to understand that they were not unclean people. Everybody seemed to have fleas in those days, albeit some more than others.

Moving the tack long distances between farms needed some planning or knowledge of the route. For one thing, the traction engine would need to take on water at various points in the journey, and you also had to be sure that any bridges could stand the weight of the engine.

'One day,' Uncle Idris told me 'I was moving the tack and on coming to a bridge that I did not like the look of I shut off the regulator on the engine, brought the tack to a stop and got down for a closer look. After inspecting the top of the bridge I went down the bank underneath the bridge to have a look at the supports. Standing on the river bank and looking up at the underside of the bridge I blanched – it only had a few baulks of timbers spanning the river from bank to bank, about the size of railway sleepers and they were so rotten you could pull chunks out of them by the handful. You could also reach up between these timbers and pull out loose stones from between them.'

'Wasn't there some timber going across the spanning timbers to form a road?' I asked.

'No,' he replied with a shake of his head.

'Go on,' I said, 'what formed the roadway then?'

'Well, the timbers spanning the river from bank to bank.'

'Yes, I understand that,' I replied, 'but what stopped the roadway from falling down between these timbers, what covered the main timbers to make a roadway?'

'I don't know. It was all so rotten and mucky, you couldn't see much of what it was. I didn't remove too many of the stones as I didn't want to make it worse. Not knowing if it would carry the weight of the tack or not, I decided to uncouple the drum and take the engine over first. Telling Harry to take up a safe position on the river bank where I could see him and where he could see underneath the bridge, so that if there was any sign of the timbers giving way, he could signal and shout to me. Uncoupling the drum and climbing back up on the engine, I drove the engine quietly over the bridge. Reaching the other side safely, I squatted the engine up and then proceeded to rope the drum across. Having got the drum almost over, with only the back wheels remaining on the last yard of the bridge, whoosh – all of a sudden down goes the bridge, drum and all with the bottom of the drum resting on the river bank and the wheels and axle down in the remains of the bridge. After shutting off the engine and nipping down to take a quick look underneath the drum, I returned, opened the regulator and roped the drum back up on safe ground. Then, taking another look round the drum to see if there was any damage done and finding everything alright, I clears off down the road,' said Uncle with a laugh.

'What about the bridge?' I asked. 'Did you do anything about the bridge?'

'Not I,' he replied. 'It was time they built another. You know, my father [Papa Price] was fording a river at one time which was in flood and on driving the engine through it the water was that deep, it put the fire out in the fire box.'

'Heck,' I said, 'I bet that made the old engine sizzle and hiss a bit.'

The Roby with its threshing tack behind, consisting of the threshing drum wagon and boulter (for tying the sheaves of straw). Farmyards were often uneven and so they also had to carry chains, blocks, jacks and a pushing pole to be able to lift and level the engine and drum.

'Yes,' he replied. We could both picture old Papa, not daunted at all, driving the engine through the flooded river with the fire hissing and roaring at his feet as it got doused. 'But mind, he had to relight the fire when he got to the other side.'

When the tack needed to be moved long distances they also had to plan the time of their move carefully, for you were not allowed to pass through towns before a certain

A view of the threshing tack whilst moving to another farm, with the Roby up front followed by the threshing drum, the wagon carrying all the kit, and the boulter.

time. While waiting you took the opportunity to attend to your fire as you were not allowed to make too much smoke while proceeding through the town. Father once told me, 'At one time there was a lot of talk that all engines had to consume their own smoke and every engine was to be fitted with a smoke consumer by law.'

Mystified as to how a smoke consumer would work, I asked, 'How did it work and what did it look like?'

'I don't know,' he answered. 'I never saw one, as in the end it never became law. Yet once when Papa Price was hard by the roadside verge with the engine taking on water, along comes a policeman. After passing the time of day the policeman, clearly thinking ahead, asked Papa Price, "Have you got a smoke consumer?"

'"Yes," said Papa without hesitation.

'"Could I see it please?" asked the policeman.

'Grandfather, without more ado said "Yes, yes, of course," opened the smoke box door and showed him the exhaust pipe. The policeman, after peering intently into the smoke box and up at the exhaust pipe, said, "Ah yes, that's alright."

'Both being happy with the day, they bide one another goodbye and went about their lawful business.'

Father once had a man working for him called Wethersbrey, an extremely strong man and loyal worker. Father was very fond of him. During one lunchtime whilst they were threshing at the Vron, near New Radnor, Wethersbrey's strength came up in conversation. Joe the Vron, as he was known, piped up saying, 'Yes, he's as strong as a horse, he eats like a horse and he stinks like a horse.' Joe and Wethersbrey did not quite hit it off. To cite how strong he was, it has been known for him to catch a 2cwt sack of corn by the neck with his two hands and swing it straight up over his shoulder onto his back.

At one time Father wanted to sink a well. He got Arthur Gore to do some water divining and locate a spot where they should start the shaft. When Father was off one day, Wethersbrey took it on himself to start sinking the well. When Father returned Wethersbrey was out of sight down the well-shaft, digging for all he was worth, but in the wrong place. Another time he started to put a post and rail fence up for Father on sloping ground. Of course it would happen when Father was not about to remind him to follow the contour of the ground. Not daunted, Wethersbrey erected a line to give a dead level for the top of the fence and dug the holes for the posts. When Father returned, Wethersbrey had finished the job off, with the posts in the ground at the top end to a depth of three foot and at the lower end only six inches in the ground, with some stakes driven down by the side of them to steady them up. It was not a first-class fencing job.

On another job where they had been threshing and were now moving to another farm, the tack was to be left just inside the gateway off the council-maintained road at the entrance onto the track that led to the farm itself. Father had to go to another farm for some reason or other and warned Wethersbrey not to move the tack until he got back: 'If I don't come back, leave the tack and go home. On no account whatsoever attempt to take the engine, drum and straw tyer [boulter] down to the farm.'

The way to this farm was over a bog by way of a road that had been built over its top. The road used to roll and dip like the waves of the sea as the engine and drum moved over it and you had to be extremely careful not to allow the engine to slip or slide off the track into the bog. Father, being familiar with the road, knew how tricky it was to get the tack over the bog. However, he was delayed and did not return that day. Wethersbrey, being most anxious to get on, climbed up onto the footplate with his mate and moved off in an attempt to get across the bog. They had not gone many yards when the engine slid sideways off the road into the bog. Down went the nearside, the hind and front wheels sinking into the mire up to the axles, with the danger of the engine going over altogether. It put the wind up Wethersbrey so much that he could not bring himself to try to extract the engine in case he tipped it over, and so the engine was left in its perilous state over the weekend. Father managed to get it off the bog on Monday by roping it to a good tree.

One day Father got himself stuck in the mud up to his knees. Finding himself well and truly fast, through no amount of easing and struggling of one foot or the other could he extract himself onto the firm ground so tantalizingly close at hand. He called for Wethersbrey to come and help, and Wethersbrey stood on firm ground, put his arms round Father and gave a tremendous heave, lifting Father clear up in the air, leaving his footwear still stuck in the mud. They had to get a spade to get his boots out.

Sadly, Wethersbrey got killed in a motorbike accident.

One of the other jobs that Father took on was sawmilling. He used to tell me about a journey that they made in the thirties to take a wagon-load of sawmilling tack to the other side of Gloucester. They went to help out a relative who had a contract there to saw up round timber.

'On the morning that we were to start out, I was up before four o'clock. Having lit the fire in the grate and put the kettle on, I then went and got steam up in the Roby.' (Father always maintained that the Roby had a nice big fire door which allowed you to put big lumps of coal in. By putting in three or four big lumps of coal, close together, he could then shut the engine down and on coming back some hours later, after being called away to some other job, he could open the fire door, spread the fire and have enough pressure on the clock to move in no time at all.) 'So having had our breakfast we set out for Gloucester, which we reached in the day. But here we got stuck on the tram lines with the wagon and portable engine on behind. I just couldn't get off the lines and there was a tram coming. The tram driver brought his tram to a stop, climbed down and walked over to see what the trouble was and said, "Don't worry, this happens quite often. I carry a bucket of sand on the tram for this sort of job." So he got the sand and sprinkled it under the wheels of the engine and we were away with many thanks to the tram driver. Going on somewhat further we reached a crossroads where there was a policeman on duty directing the traffic. We could not go fast enough for him; he was acutely waving us to come on. If we had gone as fast as that whilst out in the country, we would be summonsed.

'When we were several miles beyond Gloucester (after mounting Birdlip hill), I drew the tack over to the side and off the road, uncoupled and moved a little distance up the road to take on water. It was now twelve o'clock at night and pitch dark. Having got the engine right for taking on water and opening the valve on the water lift, I was working by feel. It was too dark to see what I was doing. While opening the valve, unbeknown to me I was unscrewing the top half of the valve, which had come lose from the main body. All of a sudden whoosh up goes the tap with steam roaring out and I heard the tap drop on the grass by the engine. I jumped down and scrabbling round in the grass, found it and hurriedly got back on the footplate and grabbed the bag off the canopy post just above the bunker. [This bag was kept there at all times in case a gauge glass broke.] I wrapped the handle of the valve in the bag, grabbed a piece of wood which I shoved under the pipe to give it support, then put the valve top and

The Roby mounting a bank heading for the Cotswolds to bring the tack home. Papa Price is in the wagon. Father, who took the photos, did most of the driving, it taking one day just to cover the 40 miles to Gloucester.

Stopped to take on water while going to fetch the tack from the other side of the Cotswolds. Uncle Idris is stood with his hand on the hind wheel and Old Tom is by the belly tank.

A view of the tack coming back from the Cotswolds. Behind the Roby is the portable engine and a wagon-load of sawmilling tack. Stood by the hind wheel are Papa Price and Uncle Idris.

bag over the body and forced it down and screwed it home. Fortunately I had saved enough steam to get the boiler filled and filled the tank so that the others who were just down the road with the tack knew nothing about it.'

'I bet her didn't half blow,' I said.

'Not half,' he replied.

'I bet there was some steam about.'

'Yes, yes,' he said nodding his head and pursing his lips. I could see by his attitude that it was a bit sticky.

'Coming home after we had completed the work, we coaled up at Gloucester Station. On this side of Ross, at about two o'clock in the morning, I drew off the road to take on water and to get some sleep, rolling myself up in a tarpaulin under the engine. But I wasn't there long. I got terrible and bitter cold. By four o'clock I was back up on the engine, stirring the fire up and was off up the road.'

'Where did the others sleep?' I asked.

'Most of them slept in the wagon. I never saw anything of them.'

'Did you get much sleep?'

'No, the noise from the engine was buzzing away in my head. That was the worst about going on a long journey with the engine. I used to have a job to get to sleep. But I have been that tired I could sleep anywhere. When some of the others took over driving so I could get some rest, many's the time I have crawled under the tarpaulin that covered the wagon and lay down in the straw to get some rest.'

'You would not get much sleep like that, would you?' I said. 'Why, wouldn't it be rough and shaking in the old wagon?'

Father looked at me with an expression speaking volumes, saying, 'Sleep, yes – when you are that tired you can sleep anywhere.'

The Roby tractor timber hauling for Bill Boulton of Titley circa 1930

One time he and Idris had to move the sawmilling tack from Llandinam over to Bridgnorth to set up a new sawmill. They set out with Father driving his beloved Roby (a steam-powered tractor), with the portable engine (with its chimney lowered and resting on the bracket above the cylinder) and wagon full of tack coupled on behind. With a blast up the chimney and a toot on the whistle they

These photographs were taken at either Cerist, Llandinam or Bridgnorth.
Top and middle right: Photographs taken in 1932 and 1935 respectively. Once sawn, all the timber had to be stacked. On the left in the middle photograph you can just see the wheel of the timber carriage. Top left: Sawn timber ready for taking away. Father is standing on the lower stack. Lower left: This photo of around 1928-1930 shows Uncle Idris.
Lower right: Father sharpening a circle saw. My sister is standing on the pile of wood to be used for firing up the engine. This photograph would have been taken in 1936.

Father working the handle on the rack bench. The two men in the background are Old Tom and Uncle Idris. The pile of sawdust in the lower photograph represents about two days' work; Father said they used to have two lorry-loads of sawdust a day. Father is second from the right holding a mug.

When sawing was done in a sawpit, with one sawyer on top of the tree and one below, the man on top of the tree was known as the top sawyer and was looked up to as a notch above the bottom sawyer. Anyone wanting to add a bit of prestige to someone, whatever their job or station in life, would say, 'He's a top sawyer', and if they wanted to belittle anyone they would say, 'He's only a bottom sawyer.' The top sawyer had the responsibility of keeping the saw straight with the aid of a soot mark on the tree which was made by springing a taut line against the tree, the line itself having first of all been doused in soot. As the saw only cut on the downward stroke, the bottom sawyer had all the sawing to do and most of the hard work. He also had all the sawdust falling down into the pit with him. There was still some pit sawing being carried out in different places in Father's young days, but not by our folks. They knocked it all on the head with their steam sawing.

moved off, Uncle Idris going on ahead of them in the car to locate the watering places for the engine.

Idris spotted a small bridge over a brook which might prove a good watering place. It so happened that there were a number of young boys playing about by the brook and as Uncle stopped the car and got out to inspect it they asked him 'Are you a German?'

Top right: The 8 horsepower Marshall sawing at Cerist.
Left: The end of the push bench and an old wooden barrow can be seen in this photograph, I think taken at Llandinam
Centre right: One of the sawmills out in the woods. Note the van just in front of the engine which Father used to live in when working away from home before he had the cabin (see also the photograph on p.84).
Lower right: Building a shed over the mill as a protection against the elements.

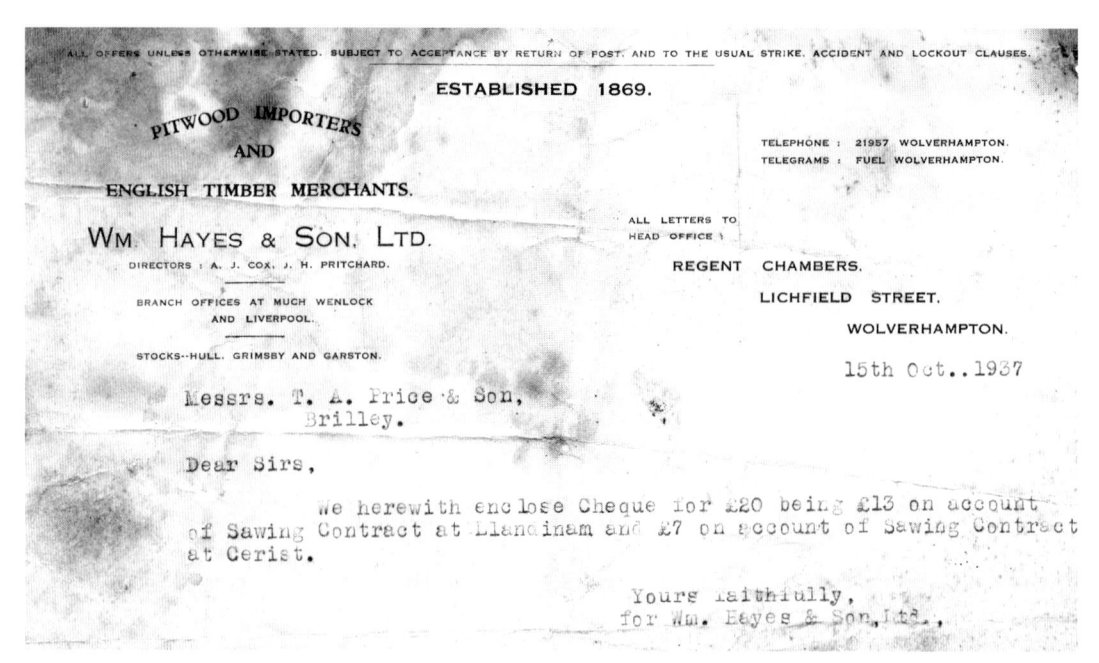

A letter that accompanied a cheque in payment for sawing work at Llandinam and Cerist, the latter between Llanidloes and Trefglwys on the B4569. Father worked there each year between 1930 and 1937.

'Yes,' he replied, pointing into the distance at the engine and tack coming along. 'You see that engine and our big gun coming along behind it?' he asked them. The boys took one look at the engine and portable bearing down towards them, with the rapid staccato of the exhaust beat and the rumbling of the wagon behind as Father piled on the steam, with the portable chimney slanting up into the air like a big gun. Without a word they fled up the road, making for the village as fast as their legs could carry them.

Father brought the tack to a halt by the bridge. It was then quickly off with the hose-pipe down into the brook, a quick fill up, a check round the tack, coil the pipe back on the engine and away again – no wasting time while taking on water. Opening the regulator, Father moved off and through the village, where all was quiet as the grave. No one came out to see what was going by. Whether the boys had run through the village shouting 'The Germans are coming' and frightened everybody into hiding we don't know. But going through most villages you generally saw someone about.

Further on, while travelling downhill into Ludlow from the Leominster side, they were held up at Ludford bridge by crowds of people and motor cars coming from Ludlow Races, toffs and all. Father told me 'They would not give way for us to get over with the tack and there was no way we could get through that crowd. They kept coming and coming and more coming. I was sat up on the engine waiting

Albert Boothroyd was an evacuee from Liverpool who was with us during the Second World War. The photograph shows him trying on his gas mask and holding a helmet. During the war when we were in bed at night, we would often be aware of the hum of planes passing overhead. One night, whilst Father was working at Wednesbury, my mother, sister, Albert and I were asleep in the bungalow when we became aware of the hum from what sounded like two German planes getting ever closer. On these occasions we would hold our breath waiting for the sound to change as the planes passed overhead and continued heading back towards the Continent, but this time there was a loud explosion from a dropped bomb, and, very frightened, we waited for a second explosion. Instead, seconds later, came a terrific noise as of hailstones rattling on the roof, then all was quiet apart from the noise of the planes receding in the distance. We hoped it wouldn't rain in the night for we felt that holes must have been made in the roof. As soon as it was light in the morning we went outside to have a look. The bomb had dropped into a field about 450 yards away, leaving a much smaller hole that we had imagined from the noise. It had sent a plume of dirt into the air, and it was part of this that had fallen onto the roof and left not a mark. The bomb crater was filled in many years later.

and waiting. Uncle Idris had soon had enough of it, and walked across the bridge in the middle of the road with one hand raised shouting, "Stop, stop you there, we want to get across this bridge. Here we are working on government work and you lot are just playing about. Don't you know there is a war on?" So he walked to the other side of the bridge and stopped the whole crowd of them.'

One of the contracts Father had for sawmilling was at Coedmynach Wood, Rhayader, where he worked for two years. This was just after the war when he had Albert to help him, and I would spend several weeks there in the school holidays. Albert had been an evacuee from Liverpool who had been placed with Father, but who enjoyed living with us so much that sometimes after he was sent back to Liverpool, he would escape and come back. In the end he worked for Father until he was called up for National Service.

As the mill was to be set up on sloping ground, Father, Uncle Idris and Albert had to cut part of the bank away in order to obtain enough level ground on which to put the engine that would drive the saw. This was all pick and shovel work, no digger in those days. It proved somewhat more difficult to secure enough ground for the rack bench, which needed the same requirements. So on the lower side of the site they built a timber frame to carry the bench, covering the framing over with oak boards. All the boards and timber for the shed and floor was sawn on the site. One handy thing about the rack bench being raised above ground level on the downhill side was that you could walk into the sawpit, shovel the sawdust straight into the barrow and wheel it away. No getting down into the pit and having to throw the sawdust up and out. The sawdust was cleaned out when the tack was shut down, very often while Father was putting some dinner on the table for us. It was a nice easy job on a summer's evening, but it was not so pleasant when it was raining. Talking of rain, I don't think I've ever seen such a place for rain. Then they also had to erect the cabin in which we stayed in during the week, just returning home at weekends.

While setting up the mill there was no sawn timber going out, so no money coming in. It was therefore a case of get the engine and rack bench fixed up and start sawing, building the shed over the engine and rack later as time allowed. I enjoyed the setting up of the mill: getting the engine into position, likewise the rack bench and push bench, and damming the brook so as to obtain a water supply for the engine. After they created their dam, Father and Uncle also directed into the pool that they had created the water from a galvanized iron pipe that supplied a Mr. Meredith. However, the brook was the other side of the road from where the mill needed to be located, and several yards below it, which meant that the water had to be pumped up to the storage tanks which were alongside the mill itself, and this required a second engine. From the tanks the water was fed by gravity to the tub by the engine whereupon she could drink to her heart's content. When Mr. Meredith came with his bucket to fetch water for his cottage he used to try and tell us it was much better to pump water by hand, as he used to do.

All this preparation was for that first great steaming day, when we opened the firebox door to light the fire, after first checking the water in the glass, oiling up all round, then watching the needle on the gauge rising steadily, and over all the sound of the file rasping on the saws as Father puts an edge on the teeth. Then opening the regulator and the old engine heaves a long awaited sigh as if shaking off a great lethargy. The crank begins its first majestic cycle and the engine starts rocking to and fro, chuntering at the chimney, pouring out life, power and warmth into the mill. We stand back admiring the old engine in all her working glory, oil-stained and weather-beaten. The sound and the movement is music to our ears, the likes that no orchestra could deliver for us. At the first movement of the crank we have already checked on the belts and saws and now our eyes stray back towards them. Everything is all in order and so we turn away to other tasks, highly pleased at the satisfying sight, sound and smell of steam in our midst. Soon we will be sawing with the sawdust pouring down into the pit in a never-ending stream. Soon the work will settle into an enjoyable routine.

My father used a little one and a half horsepower Fairbanks Bulldog open crank oil engine belted up to a pump to pump water up from the dam to the supply tanks

The engine and rack bench at Coedmynach wood.
I am stood closest to the engine, and a few yards from me is Uncle Idris.

at the mill. However, the little Fairbanks used to be somewhat troublesome. If for any reason it stopped while hot, it would sometimes start up again with the first few turns of the handle, yet another time not so. Some mornings it would start up first time, yet another time you could turn and fiddle for some time before you got it started. I think Mr. Meredith enjoyed it when we had trouble starting it, telling us that hand pumping was much more reliable.

One morning when the little Bulldog was being obstinate, not having the time to waste on this lark, Father said 'I'll go and get the six horse Fairbanks' which was always a good starter under all conditions.

'I'll come with you to help,' I ventured, knowing the weight of that engine.

'No, you stop here,' he said. The 'No' was definite. Father was putting into practise our own safety rules. Should anything happen to Uncle while he was off, I would be here to get help.

So that evening after work Father heads for home, some thirty miles away, in his 1936 car. After we saw Father off down the road, Uncle gives me a nod and indicated with his hand for me to follow him. We hurry off down to the dam and the Bulldog, to make the most of the remaining light as the evening was drawing in.

Keeping our jackets on in the cooling twilight as the nip in the air was biting, we proceeded to remove the points from the engine in order to clean them. How peaceful it was around us with the greenery of the oak trees leaning over us, the water from the spout making ripples in the pool on which gently rocked the model boat that I had made, and the smell of the damp earth coming up from the ground to meet us. The sound of the babbling brook and the tinkling of the water as it fell into the pool, I could not hear, but by resting my hand on certain places I could feel the vibration of the sound. I looked at Uncle and wondered how much he could hear as he refitted the points. Could he hear a dog barking in the distance, or some sound from the valley down below us? Were there any birds singing?

I was about to ask him when he moved back from the engine with an 'Alright,' indicating to me that I was to swing the engine. Grasping the handle and putting it on the end of the crankshaft, I glanced at Uncle who was holding the induction valve open. With a nod from him and with my jacket tails a-flying, I flayed at the starting handle, ever mindful to watch out that it did not fly off and smack me on the cheek or kneecap. Shhu, shhu, shhu, went the exhaust. I had got up to speed, Uncle took his finger off the valve, the exhaust note changed, and I could feel the compression. Come on, keep turning, keep turning, bang shhu, shhu, bang shhu bang. I stand back, having retained the handle. Bang, bang, bang, bang, we're off. Bang, bang, bang, bang. I could hear this, it sounded wonderful. The big end whirled, the fly-wheels spun, the push rod moved backwards and forwards. The point lever clicked, the induction valve snortled in and out, the engine danced and the smoke drifted up and round me.

Uncle was now moving to put the belt on. The exhaust note deepens as the load comes on the engine. We stand back to survey the engine and pump working, with the belt going endlessly round. Uncle cocks his head on one side, purses his lips and squints his eyes to listen to the sound of the pump. I freeze, standing stock still, watching his face for any sign of expression that would tell me what is happening. The silence came down around us as I waited.

'Is it pumping alright?' I asked.

'Yes,' he said, with a curt nod of his head. 'I will go and have a look in the tank.'

And so we filled the tanks up and retired to the warmth of the cabin for the night, partaking in some supper and sitting down by the old tortoise stove. While Uncle listened to the wireless I buried myself in a book. Eventually we retired to our bunks, dousing the lamp for the night, leaving only a red glow from the damper at the bottom of the stove as a source of light.

As usual next morning, I heard no sound to awaken me. Uncle, who had been up betimes, came back into the cabin, stomping on the floor, shouting and shaking the bunk, saying 'Come on get up, your dad will be here before long'. He then makes his way back out, pausing by the door to say 'Come on' by jerking his thumb over his shoulder towards the open doorway. I scramble out of my bunk as he retreats, leaving the door open behind him. The clear cold mountain air makes me shiver as it drifts into the cabin while I scramble into my clothes. I shut the door and make what I can of my breakfast. Brrr. I can't wait to start the day. Hurriedly finishing my breakfast I get up from the table and let myself out through the cabin door, making my way over to the mill and the welcoming warmth of the engine.

I glance at the pressure gauge and at the water glass, take a peek at the fire to see that Uncle has got a good fire on, then make my way on round the engine down to the rack bench, where Uncle is hard at work sawing away.

I try to make myself useful by putting the wedge in the cut to stop the timber pinching the saw as the tree comes down the bench towards me, every now and again hurrying off to the engine to throw a few more slabs on the fire and so the time moves happily along.

After what seems a short time, Father appears with the Morris hauling a trailer with the Fairbanks securely roped on. I look at the Fairbanks and wonder how much trouble he had loading it up single-handed, as it was not on a wheeled carriage but a solid oak frame, which meant that it would have to be pinch-barred all the way out of the shed and up the planks onto the trailer.

Albert and I at Coedmynach, with the 10 horsepower Ruston Hornsby, engine no.52623.

And so they carried on sawing, with me helping as much as I could, for the best part of the week. I was not there when they swapped engines, which meant more work sliding it down the bank to the dam. When I returned they had got the Fairbanks in place, and from that day forward there was no more trouble pumping water.

Among my jobs I had to keep an eye on the fire and water in the steam engine. I would also go down to the dam to the Fairbanks engine, top up the lubricator, squirt a few drops of oil here and there, cast my eye over the belt and pump, top the cooling water up if required, judge how the water was lasting out in the dam and see everything was alright. I found it all a very pleasant way in which to spend my time. It saved Father or Uncle going down to check up on things and allowed them to keep on sawing without breaking off. Sawing was all important. They were paid by the cubic foot of sawn timber, so had to keep hammering away at it.

Of course Father and Uncle would keep a weather eye on me and would come round to the engine to see how I was managing. Stopping by the hind wheel they would give me an enquiring look with the rise of the eyebrows and a slight upwards movement of the head. I would nod my head in return, keeping eye contact to say everything's okay. They would look up towards the pressure gauge and water glass, give me a nod and hurry back down to the rack bench. No words were used between us and it was over in seconds. I was to report if the water was getting low in the glass or if I wanted some more slabs sawn. Eventually I operated the pump and thus kept the boiler full.

I would also have a go at sawing a few slabs on the push bench. But I did not overdo it. I could see that they did not like to see me using the bench, as I was somewhat young for the task.

Knowing that they were keeping an eye on me and on everything else, on more than one occasion I would take a little walk for a change to see something that interested me, such as looking for a bird's nest, and take too long on my little jaunt. On hurrying back I would find Father or Uncle throwing slabs into the firebox with a stern look on their face. No words were spoken and no notice was taken of me, except a significant look straight in the eye followed by another significant look at the pressure gauge with its falling needle, their glance coming back to rest on me. The last slab would be pushed into my hands and they would indicate that I was to put it in the firebox as they turned away and hurried off back to the rack bench, leaving me to put in the slab and shut the fire door. Mortified and humbled at this lack of care on my part, I made sure that they could see me for the rest of the day trying to do my part.

But they would always let me have time for myself, as you're only young once.

Even with the new engine in place, having to pump the water up to the tanks to the mill was a nuisance, and in any event the supply running into the dam was none too great during spells of dry weather. It would obviously have been most helpful and simpler if we could obtain water uphill from the mill. It would act as an extra supply and would need no pumping. So one evening after work, Father and Uncle, with me tagging along, set out to search for water and were successful in locating a spring some ninety yards above the mill. The spring was all covered with fern and grass, and only the dampness of the area gave a clue that there was water there.

One afternoon a few days later when they needed to rope some more timber into the stack by the mill, they shut the tack down an hour or so before tea, so Albert and I walked across from the engine shed with Albert shaking the sawdust off his shoulders and brushing himself down. We paused a few yards from the cabin door, savouring the clean fresh air, the peace and tranquillity amongst the oak trees and fern of this late autumn afternoon. Already the feeling of evening was creeping in amongst us. With the engine and saws at rest and the urgency of the day's sawing fading away, the peace of the coming evening was stealing over us. But then I glimpsed Uncle starting to busy himself at some other task, so the day's work was not over yet.

All of a sudden Father came bustling over and said to Albert, 'Get the pick, shovel and spade to dig a hole up there,' pointing uphill in the direction of the spring.

'What? I,' shouts Albert (the peace of the moment evaporating), 'not another hole?'

'Yes,' replied Father smiling.

'Heck,' said Albert. 'I've dug up the side of the rack bench, I've dug and dammed the brook, I've dug the sawpit hole, the closet hole, I've been doing nothing else since I've been here but dig holes. Where will it all end?' he shouted, consternation showing all over his face.

The look on his face and his words struck me as extremely funny and I burst out laughing. Albert looked at me and started laughing too. Father turned to face me with amusement showing on his face, and said, 'You go with him.'

'Twas an hour or so before tea as Albert and I shouldered our tools, the spade, pick shovel and iron bar. I was looking forward to some good healthy digging in the clean sweet earth and I always enjoyed Albert's company. We made our way through the fern and trees up the bank to the source of the spring. Dropping our tools we paused to regain our breath and looked back down towards the mill below us. We could see the half-completed shed over the engine and rack bench, with the trees waiting to be roped up to the bench. The tractor with the two-pointed anchors of the winch pierced the air. I could almost see the wire ropes and chains lying on the ground. Casting my eyes a little to the right they rested on the cabin with its door open and the stove pipe sticking up through the roof with a wisp of smoke slowly ascending into the still, still air. Yes, it was a glorious evening and good to be alive. Beyond the cabin, on the other side the road was the faithful old Morris car waiting to transport us home on Friday night.

We could also see Father and Uncle, oh so very busy, bobbing about in and out of the mill, in and out of the cabin. 'What are they doing?' we asked one another. 'They're looking awfully busy, aren't they?' said Albert.

Turning to our task, we stomped about in the knee-high fern and soft squelchy ground underneath to locate the spring. It was somewhat difficult to say just where it was as there was no bubbling

Part of the felled wood at Coedmynach near Rhayader, not far from the dams, ready to be sawn up.

up of water, more like dampness seeping up and spreading out. Father arrived on the scene and agreed that I would open up the ground where we thought the spring was to form a catch pit, making a dam on the downhill side, while Albert would move some yards downhill and start digging a hole to act as a reservoir, also forming a dam on the downhill side. As Father made his way back down to the cabin, we got down to the job in hand. Driving our spades in we levered out the soggy earth, raising a damp mossy smell with each spadeful. It was a totally different smell from our red earth in Herefordshire. As we settled to our labours, there was just a little crispness stealing into the air, making it just right for some good hard digging. Every now and again we would take a look down towards the cabin to see if there was any sign of our tea. The digging was now going apace and we had both got down in the ground, piling the spoil up to form a dam of our respective holes. After we had got down in the ground somewhat, we started lobbing a few mudballs at one another. We knew that this was foolish, but being that there were some trees between us, it required great skill to gently toss a nice soft mudball over and catch the other on the back of the neck as he was bending to his labours. It was not long until we got down to it in earnest. With plenty of mudballs zooming about, things soon hotted up, and we took cover in our reservoirs, which had now become dug-outs. Images of the war coming into my mind, I fell to and under cover made plenty of ammunition ready for the big push. Popping my head up over the top of the trench to spy out the land, smack, I got one straight in the face. Feeling mortally wounded, I was very glad for Albert to come and swill my face down with muddy smelly water from out of the bottom of the pit, and we agreed to call off hostilities before any real damage was done. Just then there was a shout from the cabin for tea (not that I heard it). But through my smarting eyes I saw Albert jerk his head up in an attitude of listening. 'Tea's ready,' he said.

We climbed up out of the pit and hared off down the bank. We went going full tilt, leaping, bounding, running through the fern and dodging the trees as if all the hounds in hell were after us. We were looking forward to our tea and having a sit down on the old wooden bench.

As we started on our tea, Father looked at my red face and watery eyes but asked no questions, so I kept my counsel. Instead I asked Father, 'What were you doing when we were digging up at the spring?' No answer was forthcoming. I really was interested to know what all the activity that Albert and I had observed was about. 'What were you doing?' I pressed. I must have phrased the question all wrong, or perhaps they were listening to the wireless and I was interrupting their programme.

Father gave me a fierce look with annoyance showing on his face. 'Getting tea,' he replied, holding my eye as if waiting for some impertinence. I glanced down the table past Uncle at Albert.

Albert was looking down hard at his plate. I could see that I had got it wrong somewhere. Turning back to Father, who was still holding my eye, I said, 'Oh, I just wondered, as you looked very busy popping about and in and out of the cabin and the mill, didn't they, Albert?'

'Yes, yes that's right,' agreed Albert, laughing and violently nodding his head up and down.

I never did discover what else they had been up to apart from getting the tea.

Averting my gaze from Father's piercing eye, I looked out through the window which was directly in front of me. My glance travelled between the oak trees to the edge of the wood and beyond to the little green field and cottage where Mr. and Mrs. Meredith lived. He was a retired smallholder, an old man now. He used to come over to the cabin for a talk some evenings and he was indeed a very interesting person to talk to. He told Father that he worked on every dam that was built in the Elan Valley bar the last one. He related many humorous stories. For instance, when the stonemasons were dressing the stone in the quarry they would all be plying their hammer and chisels. The sound of them tinkling round the quarry in harmony, created a kind of music. If any inexperienced person decided to try his hand at stone dressing, his efforts struck great discord in the tinkling harmony. The masons, on hearing such a sound, would stop work and would not start again until that person had put down the tools and left the scene. (Father once asked Mr. and Mrs. Meredith to come to dinner and tea one Saturday afternoon, assuring them that he would fetch them and take them back. So they spent a Saturday afternoon with us and we took them back to their cottage after tea that evening. I think they thought it was a long trip indeed.)

After tea we made our way back up to the spring. The water was now seeping into our pits and we had to bail out before we could start digging again, every now and again breaking off from our labours to bail more water out. We carried on until it became dark, when we called it a day, climbed out of the pits and made our way slowly between the oaks with just enough light left to pick our way through the fern towards the welcoming light from the cabin, with the sparks lifting up out of the stove pipe, stopping in the darkness of the engine shed, the great black bulk of the engine looming over us as we removed our muddy boots and overalls.

I did some more digging the next day on my own, with Father coming up to see how I was getting on. As it was now Friday, at the end of the day we headed for home, whilst Albert remained at the cabin over the weekend to carry on digging. The water from the spring was eventually piped down to the storage tanks with galvanized iron pipes.

The wooden cabin which my father erected at Coedmynach wood was fifteen feet long by ten feet wide, built in sections so that you could dismantle it and transport it from job to job. It was where Father, Uncle, Albert or old Tom (who followed Albert) and myself, when I was there, lived all week. In the middle of the cabin was a tortoise stove. On top of the stove was the kettle. Bolted to the base of the stove pipe was an iron shelf made out of two angle irons to stand the teapot on to keep the tea hot. All cooking was done on top of this stove – mostly breakfast and boiled meat for dinner. Behind the stove was a wooden stand with a bowl of water for washing one's hands and face. This was only brought inside in extremely cold weather. At all other times, we washed outside by the door under the porch roof by the light of a guttering candle stuck on the ledge. This was awful on a cold, dark winter's night, more so if it was raining and the wind was keenly cutting into you – and you were expected by Father to have a good wash before settling down in the cabin for the evening on those long, dark winter nights. At least a hot kettle of water was available, or some hot water from the engine, but it was surprising how quickly a tin bowl in the open air cooled the water. Your hands and face would glow from the wash and being rubbed dry with an old rough but clean bit of sacking, before finishing off with a towel.

Our meals consisted of bread and cheese, cold meat and potatoes with home-made chutneys and pickled onions. Real savoury foods, including home-baked cake, apple and gooseberry tarts, the like of which you don't find today, with eggs and home-cured bacon for breakfast sizzling in the pan on top of the stove, filling the cabin with a mouth-watering aroma, and maybe a rice pudding for afters at dinner time, spiced with bay leaves or nutmeg. It was all washed down with strong tea, very often with no milk or sugar in it, if sugar was in short supply.

There was to be no filth or untidiness in the cabin. If anybody erred it was not long until they were told to rectify matters.

On entering the cabin, on the left-hand side was Uncle's bed. On the opposite side was the table, the bench and food cupboard. Further on along the same side was Father's bed, opposite which was a bunk bed. Albert or old Tom slept in the bottom bunk and I in the top bunk. When old Tom left I took to sleeping in the bottom bunk, as it was terribly hot up in the top bunk at night with the stove going full blast, and cold in the morning if the fire had gone out.

Between the bunk and Father's bed was a chest of drawers in which to keep spare clean clothes, also blankets, First Aid kits and so forth. On top of the chest was a wireless. Between the bunk and Uncle's bed was a desk for what office work was to be carried out. For daylight illumination there was a window in the middle of each side wall. At night the cabin was lit by paraffin lamp and in latter years by Tilley lamp.

Having had our tea in the evening, we would settle in our usual places round the stove. Father would sit on his bunk with his back resting against the back wall, logging up the day's work using a Hoppus Ready Reckoner and bringing his diary up to date. Over by the door Uncle would be sat on his bunk doing a spell of reading, while old Tom would be relaxing on his bunk. I myself would be sat on the end of Tom's bunk up close to the stove or lying up in the top bunk reading. Looking at the wireless I would often notice that the light was glowing faintly from the dials, and gather that they were listening to a programme. After some time, judging that Father had about finished his logging, I would often venture a question about years gone by. Father and Uncle would both look at me and their eyes would take on a faraway look, going back to the days when steam ruled supreme in the land and the men on the footplate were kings indeed. Father's eyes would come back to focus on me, whilst Uncle looked up at me, shifting his gaze from the red embers in the ashpan at the bottom of the stove. My eyes darted from one to the other to catch which was going to speak first, bringing every vestige of my lip-reading skill to bear in the weak lamplight so as not to miss a golden word.

After a while, as the darkness deepened, Uncle would get up and go to the middle of the cabin by the stove, reach up and take down the Tilley lamp from its place on the hook overhead. Once lit it was hung back on its hook, the light filling the cabin and dispelling the darkness. I leaned back on my bunk in contentment, able to see again. Cosy as the darkness made the cabin, it made it extremely difficult for me to lip-read in the dim and flickering light from the bottom damper of the stove. On more than one occasion the lamp was not lit and I had to endure the long dark evenings trying to read by the light from the stove, or sat on the bench at the table making the most of the fading light through the window, then giving up as the light faded altogether and the hardness of the bench manifested itself. Going and lying on my bunk, I mustered as much patience as I could while Father and Uncle reposed on their bunks listening to the wireless. Thank goodness it did not happen very often.

The first night I shared the bunk with old Tom I was frightened to death. I woke up to find I could feel and hear a terrible noise, the sound travelling through the timbers of the bunk. The cabin was in darkness, and I could not make out what the noise was. I really thought it was the end of the world. I thought the boiler on the engine had burst and was blowing steam sky-high, and we would be on our own way up within a few seconds as the blast came rocketing through the cabin. Suddenly I realised that it was old Tom snoring. I had often heard Father talk about the crescendo that Tom made when going full blast, but it was the first time I had experienced anyone snoring. Sinking back down into the bed with blessed relief, I closed my eyes and looked forward to getting back to sleep. But it was hopeless. The roaring crescendo was coming up through the bunk. Enduring this for some time and getting furious that I was losing my sleep, suddenly I felt a clunk vibrate through the timbers of the cabin as if old Tom had busted a gut. Then everything went quiet. Thankful, I managed to drop off. Early next morning as I wearily peered down at the floor from atop my bunk, I was somewhat puzzled to see Father nip across the cabin and pick something up at the foot of Tom's bed. That explained what that clunk in the night was. He was retrieving his boot.

Later that morning, when old Tom was out of earshot, I said to my Father and Uncle, 'What a night, what a terribly noisy night.' They pulled up short, all attention and looking at me with puzzled frowns on their faces.

'What was noisy?' they both asked me.

'Old Tom,' I replied. 'He was making a terrible din.'

They started to smile, but at the same time both turned on me, saying, 'How could you hear him? You can't hear.'

'Hear him, hear him? I didn't have to hear him,' I said. 'The whole blooming bunk was vibrating like, like heck, it frightened me to death.'

After enduring several nights of being woken up by Tom's racket I found out what to do. If I gave the bunk a real good shake and disturbed him, he stopped snoring for a time, enabling me to get back to sleep. Some nights it was snore, shake, sleep, snore, shake, sleep, half the night.

Old Tom liked his beer and would get as drunk as an owl. On coming back to the cabin after an evening's drinking late at night, when

Old Tom.

everybody had retired to bed to get some well-earned sleep, he did not make a sound. You never heard him open and shut the door, walk across the boarded floor to his bunk and climb into his bed. In all the years that he worked for my folks, never once did he wake anyone on his return, only sometime later in the night when his thunderous snoring began to vibrate throughout the cabin.

Not being able to hear birdsong, nor the sound of tinkling cups and saucers or the rattling of the frying pan or kettle, I was nearly always the last one up. When I got up, Father would be frying up the breakfast on the stove and Uncle would be stirring the fire up in the engine. If Albert, before he joined the RAF, or old Tom was with us, he and Uncle might be roping some timber in closer to the rack bench. As the years passed, old Tom turned up for work less and less. No doubt he was feeling his age. Papa and Granny were dead and gone and old Tom was missing Papa sorely as he had worked for him for donkeys' years. Eventually Tom failed to turn up on Sunday nights or Monday mornings altogether.

Old Tom had always acted as the steersman on the engines and the feeder on the drum. He also kept up steam in the portable engine when they were sawing. Another of his jobs was to keep the rivets hot when they were carrying out repairs. Father used to like telling stories about old Tom, such as the one about one evening when he and Tom were miles from home with the Roby and they had brought the engine to a stop alongside a likely looking place to take on water. They had just climbed down from the footplate when out of the gloaming walks a gentleman with an 'Oi, oi, you can't take water from there', whereupon there followed a long explanation as to the reasons why. Father was taking it all in, giving the gentleman his full attention whilst old Tom carried on uncoiling the hosepipe from the engine, putting it in the water and turning the water lifter on. By the time the gentleman had finished his discourse, old Tom had filled the tanks to the brim and coiled the pipe back on the engine. So, bidding the gentleman goodnight, Father and Tom took their places back upon the engine, Father opened the regulator and with a nice full boiler and tanks they steamed off into the night, the gentleman being none the wiser that some of the coveted water was now making its way off down the road.

Another of his tales was of a time they were all working at Wednesbury, near Birmingham. One of the men, George, decided to hold a Christmas raffle for which the prize was a cockerel, which he arranged for old Tom to feather and dress as he was a dab hand at it. Tom was always black from all his engine driving, and by the time he had finished plucking and dressing, the cockerel was as black as a pot.

Tom was once offered a home by one of his relatives if he would give up his drinking, but Tom preferred his beer and his pipe. He lived to the grand old age of ninety. Poor old Tom, I missed him when he was gone. He was good company. When a General Election was taking place, if you asked him who he was going to vote for he always replied 'Guy Fawkes'.

One day at the mill at Coedmynach I was sat down with my back resting against the front wheel of the engine, which was rocking gently to and fro as she chuntered away at her work. Now and again she would bellow louder and increase her rocking motion as the going got harder when the saw bit into some hard knotty parts of the tree and the governor opened to pour more steam into the cylinder, then shutting back again to her usual gently working chunter and rocking as the workload eased off.

I was trying to get some warmth from the engine and the sun, which was rapidly losing its strength in the late afternoon. I was feeling tired and happy after some tedious work all afternoon of barking trees – removing the dirty, mud-caked, stone-encrusted bark from the trees which they had picked up while being roped along the ground down to the mill. If the bark wasn't removed, it would take the cutting edge off the saw.

The trees were in a stack waiting to be rolled down to the mill as and when required, the mill itself being just a few yards below the stack. Not far away was another stack of timber waiting to be roped up to the mill. I viewed this stack with dread. Barking trees I found was a terribly tedious job.

As I sat there with my back against the wheel, drinking in all the good things about steam, out of the corner of my eye, I could see Father and Uncle rhythmically working one of the tables of the twin rack bench backwards and forwards, sawing up the round oak timber, while a few yards away on my side was old Tom sawing up the waste slabs on the push bench as they came over his way into suitable lengths to be fed into the firebox of the engine.

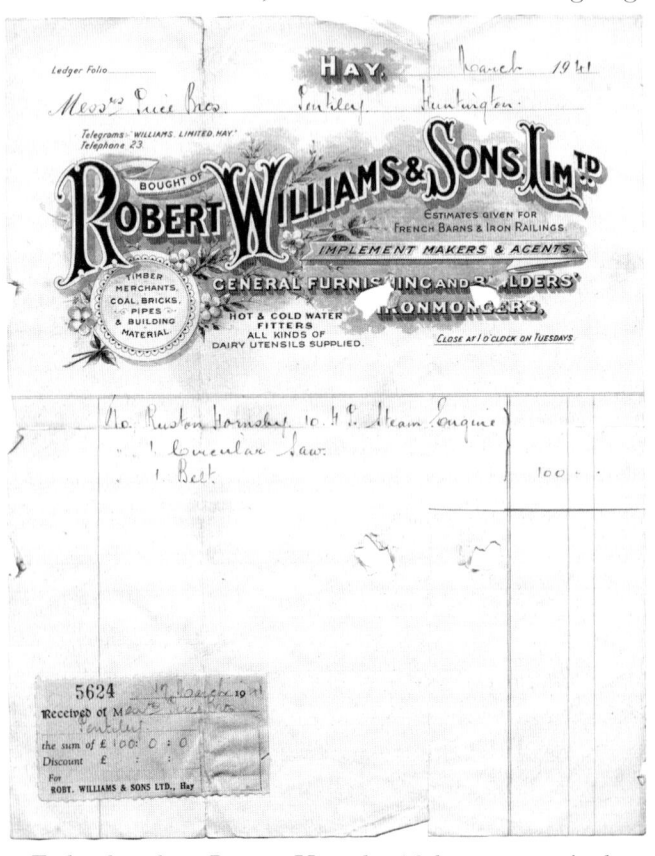

Father bought a Ruston Hornsby 10 horsepower single cylinder engine, together with a circular saw and belt at the outbreak of the Second World War, and paid for it in 1941. It went by rail to Wednesbury, where he had a sawmill sawing timber for B. Walsh Graham Ltd. This was one of the engines we used at Coedmynach.

68

Then suddenly, chuff, chuff, chuff, chuff, never before or since have I seen such power and fury unleashed in a few seconds. Cape Canaveral has got nothing on it. The motion of the engine at my back was violently increasing at a terrific rate. Springing upwards and at the same time turning to face the engine and hurriedly backing away, I was just in time to see Father getting into top gear. I never thought my old Dad had such a turn of speed. He was spinning the handle, winding back the table with the tree on it at the same time knocking the handle out of gear and leaving the table to go back under its own momentum and for Uncle to take care of, the back edge of the saw screaming and howling as it came out of the cut. Then Father ran like blazes down the side of the rack bench, disappearing past the smoke box with clouds of sawdust falling from his hat and shoulders, streaming in his wake and Uncle now came on behind, also leaving a wake of sawdust. Now old Tom came out of the blue from behind the push bench, his legging-encased calves and booted feet making bowlegged drumming as he galloped down the wooden platform. All of them were running to save the engine on which our livelihood depended. I myself was going to make a dash for the regulator, but I could see it was all being taken care of.

Jumping off the platform down the bank away from the engine to get a good view of all that was taking place, I will never forget the sight. The governor belt had broken and was lying along the top of the boiler like a flat, black, dead snake. The flywheel spokes and big end were just a blur, the eccentric rods were one solid sheet, and the speed was increasing all the time. The engine's front wheels were just

Our little 6 horsepower Ruston Hornsby. The man is Albert's brother-in-law, and above his head you can see the hollow expansion stay running between the cylinder and the crankshaft mounting which took steam off the boiler.

dancing on the spot, the back wheels were rocking and flapping like pigs' ears, while the chimney rapidly rocked as if bent on self-destruction. Out of the chimney itself spewed forth great clouds of sparks, smoke, steam and black halfburnt bits of wood almost as big as my fist, with red sparks glowing and winking in them. It was sending it all high into the sky from where it began raining down like hellfire and brimstone. It was an awesome sight, what with the rapid thump, thump, thumping of the front wheels dancing on the ground. I could feel the vibration coming up through the soles of my boots.

Father slammed shut the regulator, and held it and looked at me in an attitude of listening. For the first few seconds or so there was no visible sign of the engine starting to slow down. 'Heck,' I thought 'There's no stopping her now, she's going to run to smithereens.' I really thought the old engine was going to disintegrate, but as these thoughts flashed through my mind, the engine began to slow. It seemed a long time before she gently came to a rest, simmering away to herself as we gathered by the side of the engine to inspect the broken belt. How quiet and still it now seemed after such a display of unleashed power. I was awed by the sight I had just witnessed. It must have been over in seconds, yet I had seen so much that it seemed an incredibly long time. Father and Uncle, who had seen it all before, were taking it placidly and quietly as usual.

Father had a look at the engine to make sure everything was alright. Old Tom was making the most of the lull, carting his sawn slabs from the push bench down to his stack by the firebox door. I can still see old Tom stood just behind the hind wheel (Father and Uncle had their backs to him) looking at me, laughing all over his face, happily enjoying the respite from his labours.

The belt was easily repaired, and Uncle, with a nod of his head and a laugh, looked at Father, who smiled and returned his laugh. They both agreed that we might as well call it a day and have some tea. So we all trooped into the cabin for an early evening meal, over which events of past engines were related to me, the stove warming my back as the cooling evening air stole through the open cabin door and my eyes strained as the gathering dusk made it harder and harder for me to see to lip read. But the afternoon and evening drove home to me the lesson that Father used to repeat: 'Never leave your engine when it's working, or go too far away if you are called away unavoidably. Make sure everything is safe and secure See to the fire, water, damper and so on, and get someone on the job to keep an eye on the engine for you.' It was a lesson well learned.

Another thing he used to drive home to me was 'Never throw paraffin into the firebox or your engine in order to light the fire, even if your engine has been at rest with no fire for a day or so and there is no sign of a spark or life in the firebox. It's been known for people to open the fire door and throw some paraffin in. All is still and quiet while they fumble for a match, then whoosh, out of the firedoor comes a ball of fire that burns the hairs off their eyebrows and singes the hairs of their head. Nasty experience, always wear your cap and jacket for protection, David.'

In due course the work at Coedmynach wood came to an end. For me it was the scene of many happy times, but for Father and Uncle it was one of hardship, of cold, wet and muddy days, well finished with, as the contract was a very tough one with no chance of any price rise as it was all signed and sealed beforehand. But never once did I hear them complain. It was only years afterwards that they said to me, 'It was a very poor reward for a lot of hard work.'

But there were other, smaller sawing jobs to be done too. When Father and Uncle were working a wood not far from the foot of the Black Mountains, I often used to go along with them. The timber to be extracted was situated on the side of a very steep dingle, almost straight down in places.

On one day in particular we had been roping some timber up out of the dingle with the tractor. It was a lot of hard work pulling the rope out and walking back up this extremely steep dingle, following the tree up to the stack. Many days were wet, muggy and miserable, but this particular day was nice and sunny. We had just roped one tree up to the rack bench and Father and I were having a blow leaning on the self same tree, while Uncle Idris shifted the tractor for another pull.

'You see that house over there?' said Father, pointing to a house the other side of the dingle, about a mile or more away. The house appeared to be built into the side of the hill, about midway between the top and bottom, with a lane leading from the house down to the public road. We could often see a single figure, sometimes two figures, walking this lane.

'Yes,' I replied.

'How far would you put the house from the road?'

Casting my eye from the house to the road and back again, 'All of a mile I would think,' I answered.

'Yes I would think that,' he said. 'Have you seen the old boy who lives in the house walking that lane?'

'Yes,' I replied.'

'Have you seen the postman walking with him?'

'No, I can't say that I have. I have seen two figures walking together, but it's too far away to say if it was the postman for sure.'

The Roby and timber carriage hauling out of a field on the Nieuport estate in Almeley. This tree weighed 13 tons and the carriage sank a foot into the mud.

'Well, that would most likely be the postman,' said Father.

I settled myself more comfortably on the tree as Father paused. I cast my eyes over towards Uncle, some thirty yards away. He was hunched over the steering wheel, lurching about as he made his way further away from the rack bench. I looked back at Father who was looking at me to see if I was getting the gist of the conversation. Giving him a nod to show that I understood, he continued saying, 'Well, I've been told that the old gentleman who lives in the house by himself would walk down the lane from his house to meet the postman. If there was a letter for him, he would not take the letter off the postman at the road, but would walk all the way back up to the house with him, take the letter off him, then walk all the way back down to the road with the postman, see him out on the road, then walk back up to his house to read his letter.'

'What, all that walking just for a letter?' I said.

'Perhaps he was glad to see somebody,' said Father.

'No doubt,' I replied. 'It looks awfully lonely up there.'

'Yes and one night, when hearing a lot of rats scurrying about in the attic above him, he fired his shotgun up at the ceiling, peppering it with shot and no doubt blowing a hole in it at the same time.'

'Did it stop the rats?' I asked.

'I don't know,' he replied, laughing. 'I never heard any more about it.'

My parents with their 1949 Austin 16.

And so we turned our attention back to the job in hand, making our way up to the tractor to pull the rope out once more. I stopped and took another look at the house on the side of the hill, and felt sorry for the man who must be so lonely living by himself.

One day we were sawing in the workshop and had to get some water for the engine from the pool opposite the turning to Holborn Farm. As we stood by the side of the pool, having collected some buckets of water, and waited for the engine to warm up, Father said to me, 'I believe this is a dew-pond. It is lined out with white clay, but I don't know where in Brilley white clay could be obtained. The one place where they might have got it from is over at the clay pits Kinnerton way, but I'm not sure now if it is white clay.' Changing his line of thought, he said 'You see those two clumps of rushes in the middle there?'

Peering hard at the rushes, I nodded an affirmative.

'Well, those reeds were left there in memory of Queen Victoria's Jubilee. That was when the pool was last cleared out. Also there used to be a causeway from where that telephone pole is now out into the middle of the pool. Davies of Holborn built it so that he could back the horse and cart out to the middle of the pool to enable him to ladle clean water into the barrel on the cart.'

'Well,' I said, 'would the water be any cleaner in the middle of the pool than at the side?'

'I shouldn't think so,' he replied, laughing. 'I was going to clean the pool out myself at one time, but I never got round to it. I was going to put an engine each side of the pool and rope an old open-ended cart through, just to get the loose mud out. But you would have to be careful cleaning out this dew-pond, as if you took the clay lining off the bottom and sides, you would spoil it and it would not hold water the same.' He then proceeded to explain to me how a dew-pond was made and how it worked.

'The pool was most likely made for animals to drink out of up on the hill when it was all open ground, before the hill was divided up with hedges in 1812. It was always very handy for watering the engines. We were very hard up for water in 1921 or 1922. It was a very dry spell, so we had to get some water for the engines up on the Common [where there is another pool]. We just managed to get enough water to keep going.' This was the only time I can remember the pool going dry until 1976. The mud was baked that hard, you could walk across it.

The last sawing job that my Father and Uncle did with steam, as this way of sawing up round timber was going out of use, was at a wood just outside Rhayader by the side of the river Wye. It was only Father and Uncle on this job, and I went when I could. Papa was dead and gone, old Tom had aged and given up work, and we could no longer afford to keep men working for us. Those days were long gone.

It was a lot of work to move the tack to a new site. The shed had to be taken down, the rack bench dismantled and packed up, the engine drained, moved and readied for the road. The saw pit was filled in, the dam destroyed, water pipes taken up, with all the tools such as crosscut saws, axes, wedges, chains and wire ropes packed up and taken to the new site. And while this work was going on there was no pay coming in.

The standing timber and the ground on which it grew at the new site belonged to a Mr. Price, from whom they purchased the timber. It was a somewhat difficult site to work. At the top of the site was a mainline railway station from which the ground sloped down to a private road, and from the road it carried on sloping sharply down to the Wye itself. On no account was the road to be blocked by falling timber, or the surface torn up. There was no room to set the mill up on the same side as the wood, so it was set up the other side of the river in a meadow right on the riverbank, with the cabin hard by, underneath a fir tree. As this was most likely the last sawing job out in the woods that we would carry out, no shed was to be built over the mill. Only a tarpaulin over the fire-box end of the engine was to be erected. It was sad indeed to see the tack out in the wet.

The meadow where the mill was set up had very good access from the road, which greatly facilitated the easy removal of the sawn timber. Access between the wood and the mill was by way of a narrow footbridge high above the water. Should we want the tractor one side of the river or the other, Uncle had to drive it through the ford, which was just down river from the footbridge. However, should the river be running high, it was impossible to drive the tractor through and since this was the only means of fording the river, an eye had to be kept on the caprices of nature.

For me it was an altogether most picturesque site. With the old engine, the river running by the cabin underneath the fir tree and now and again the railway engine thun-

This is the height of the timber, Douglas fir and spruce, they were felling and sawing at Rhayader. Uncle Idris is stood at the bottom ready to put the sink in. Beautiful were the trees to behold. They towered high into the sky, reaching unbelievable heights, while the branches themselves were the size of ordinary trees. It was almost a sin to fell such wonderful giants of the forest, and the girth at the butt was often more than thirty-six inches in diameter.

In the background behind the lady, a Miss Lovegrove, is the little narrow footbridge that we used to cross from the cabin and the mill to the wood. The bridge no longer exists.

dered along, leaving in its wake the wonderful smell of steam which put a tang in your nose.

Once the tack was all in place, the next job was boxing the butts of the trees. The axing of the butts of the trees all round the girth and removing any spurs made for a tidy job and better felling. Also they sat better on the rack bench. Later on came the actual work of felling. First of all it was decided where the tree was to be dropped, taking into account the line of the fall and any other trees in the vicinity. So, having whetted the edge of the axe and got an edge like a razor, then gripping the handle and raising the axe about the shoulder, a start was made to put the sink in. Swinging the axe and making the chips fly all round the base of the tree is a most satisfying practice, building it up to a fine art to be able to put the edge of the axe just where you want it with hardly ever a miss. Some of the sinks I've seen looked as if they had been planed with a smoothing plane, hardly a mark from the axe being left on the timber. This was real craftsmanship in action.

Having decided which tree to fall and put the sink in for the direction of the fall itself, there was only one way to fall the trees on this site and that was parallel to the railway, the road and the river, but at the same time falling them away from the railway for safety sake, with just the tops of the trees touching the edge of the road when they were down actually lying slantwise on the bank. Picking up the crosscut saw, Father and Uncle gets down behind the sink in order to start the felling cut. Because the ground was sloping steeply, the topside man knelt on a sack to keep his trousers dry, whilst the lower side man was able to work from a stooping position. They fell to, with the saw whipping backwards and forwards quickly and lightly. It was a great sight to see the sawdust coming out of the end of each cut, great ribbons of shavings as the rakers of the saw fetched them out into a little pile of sawdust each side of the tree.

Father looks up at me grinning and shouts 'We're off!', and Uncle casts a sardonic grin at me over his shoulder. They both turn back to their work, gaining a little more speed as they buckle to after that momentary lapse. I stand back to survey the scene. How beautiful it all looks. The very air is like a balm on the face, filling the lungs with the liqueur of life and the day bodes well. I lean against the railway fence and peer down along the shining metals below me and at the black sleepers with a wet greasy streak from the engine running along the middle of them, wondering when the next train will be along, and hope and pray that the tree will fall as planned. God forbid that it or any should ever go across the line.

I run my glance down to the orange tractor with its winch waiting for action, my eyes travelling on down to the river in all its beauty. I bring my eyes back upwards and look through the wood at the sunlight twinkling and dancing amongst the trees, the light brown ribbon-like bark on the branches of the Scots pine peeling here and there, the green pine needles, and the brown cones peeping out of the mat of brittle dry needles underfoot as they float on a thick damp carpet of their long-fallen brothers. I breathe in great lungfulls of the sharp fresh pine smell intermingling with the damp smell of the earth, and admire in wonder the soft green cushion of moss on the hard grey rocks. It is beauty indeed.

I move down and pass the sawyers, the hammer and wedges which they drive into the cut to take the weight off the saw, the sound of the hammer ringing round the woods. I look at the tree once more. How beautiful it is! Poor tree, I wonder who had the foresight to plant you all those years ago. A movement from the sawyers arrests my attention. Looking quickly at them, I see they are both looking at me without stopping work, frowning. I should not let my attention wander. With a curt nod of his head and indicating with his hand, 'Drive the wedges in,' says Father. They both turn rapidly back to their work, looking intently at the cut and increasing the speed of the saw. Perhaps the saw is binding a little, I think to myself, grasping the short handle sledge I drive the wedges in, taking careful aim so at the same time I can peer up to the top of the tree to see if it jerks over. Putting the hammer down by the tree, I step back and once again looking through bowls of bark I can see part of a tree that overhangs the cabin, our shelter and warmth for the night. It is as if we are working and living in another age. Outside of our circle is a more modern world.

Looking back at the sawyers and the now considerable pile of sawdust each side of the tree, so as not to be caught out again I hurry forward to drive the wedges in some more. Soon Father and Uncle pause, it's time to put the rope on, the wire rope leading back down to the winch on the tractor. A certain amount of it has already been pulled out, and the end of the rope with its C hook coupling is lying at the foot of the tree ready to be fastened thirty foot or so above where we stand.

Putting the rope on the tree at this stage was one of the things that Father and I did not agree on. But I was always allowed to voice my opinion, even if it did not carry much weight. It was like this, Father always wanted to do so much work before putting the rope on, such as put the sink in and saw so much of the felling cut. I always wanted to put the rope on first, before doing any of these things, fearful that the tree would otherwise go over as the rope was being attached.

Uncle makes his way down to the tractor to pull out some more rope from the winch. We had to drag the rope out from the winch in stages as it was too heavy to drag out in one long length. To make it easier we used to sling it over low branches or an already fallen tree. This made it much easier than trying to pull it along the ground.

Meanwhile Father rests the ladder against the tree, and picking up the end of the rope with the C hook, climbs quickly up, dragging the rope up with him, while I pull up the slack from Uncle, who is now some distance away with the rope over his shoulder walking towards me, bringing the rest of the rope with him. I continue hauling in and paying up the rope to Father, who has now disappeared up amongst the branches. Uncle appears at the foot of the tree bent double, breathing a little harder, and slings the rope off his shoulder, letting out a long 'phew' of breath, at the same time peering upwards through the branches.

I now climb up the ladder and onto one of the branches to help to pull up the heavy rope, always wondering if the bottom of the tree is giving way as it sways in the wind. With a good foothold and hooking one arm over a branch, I pass the rope upwards, keeping a sharp eye on Uncle for directions. Suddenly the rope stops its upwards movement and Uncle is waving and saying 'Stop'.

Uncle is stood in an attitude of listening, so I watch him intently yet relax against the trunk, drinking in all the good things of nature. The gentle breeze moves amongst the branches. The fragrance of the pine drifts around me. Then Uncle's head tilts slightly to one side, his head and face whips up towards me and he raises one arm upwards, indicating for me to haul up whilst his lips say 'A bit more, a bit more, a bit more, stop!' We wait a few more moments. Then he looks up towards me saying, 'Alright, come down', at the same time waving his arm downwards. Letting go of the rope gently as not to cause any sudden jerk or movement on it and thus put Father in danger by pulling him off balance should he be holding it, I climb down thankfully. Reaching the ground I give Uncle a wan smile, saying, 'The tree was swaying like heck, I thought we were going over many times.' Uncle, with both eyebrows raised, laughs at my discomfort.

Turning away from him and kneeling down at the butt of the tree, I put my finger in the sawn cut. I can feel the squeezing and slacking on my finger as the cut opens and closes with the movement of the tree. 'Feel that,' I say as he is still smiling nonchalantly.

By now Father has come down from the upper branches and joined us. I impart my thoughts to him, with my finger still in the cut, and he too kneels down and puts his finger in. The sound of silence gathers round us while the pressure tightens and eases on my finger. 'That's nothing' he says looking at me and laughing at my fears as we raise ourselves up, brushing the pine needles from the kneecaps of our trousers.

I look at them intently. They both return my gaze, holding my eyes steadily. 'Ah well, I suppose it isn't,' I say. 'But what if there was a strong wind?'

They look at me, nodding sagely as if to say 'We would have taken that into account.' The looks on their faces, the tilt of their heads, the stance of their bodies and the slight movement say it all for them: 'We know what we are about, so watch and learn.'

Kneeling down at the butt of the tree once more, they continue sawing. Every now and again I drive the wedges in and the sound of the saw drifts over the peaceful scene. There comes an atmosphere of tranquillity, calm and peace that acts like a balm on my soul.

After a while Uncle goes down to start the tractor. So with a nod from Father I take over and after we have done some more sawing he says, 'You see, it hasn't gone yet. Drive the wedges in a bit more.'

Out of the corner of my eye I can see Uncle cranking the old Ford into life. Some smoke ejects from the exhaust pipe as the engine fires. Uncle reaches sharply round the radiator to work the choke. We continue sawing, gradually reaching the final stages of the felling cut, Uncle tightening the rope to give the tree a pull in the right direction. Father is driving the wedges in as I move back a yard or so, remembering that the butt of the tree is the safest place to be when felling timber. The cut opens wider, the tree is on its way. No more help can be given by the wedges and as they fall loose Father lifts the crosscut saw out of harm's way and steps back.

Together we watch the spectacular display of the tree going down. Slowly, slowly there starts a slight movement in the direction of the fall. At first hardly perceptible, then gathering speed, and as it goes the cut at the butt was opens wider. The top of the tree cuts an arc across the sky. The sound of splintering pervades loudly over all. So high is the tree, it seems to take an incredibly long time to fall. As it hits the ground with a resounding gruuuuuuunch, some of the branches are driven deep down into the earth. The butt rears up, rolls a little and lies still. The branches whip about, then

Some of the timber being felled and sawn near Rhayader in 1953-4.

wave and settle into stillness. It was over, its long great life finished. The silence settles round us.

We both pause for a moment where we stand. It is a sad sight to see such beauty lying forlornly on the ground. We move off into the foliage of the tree to free the rope so that Uncle can wind it back up onto the drum on the tractor, as not to foul the axes when lopping the branches off the tree. While Father and Uncle get busy with this job I count the annual rings on the stump. Looking back, I pause and think, was it really one hundred and twenty rings I counted, but I have carried this figure in my head ever since the day I counted them.

When time allowed, the wood chips were bagged up and carried down through the wood along the road by the river, over the bridge and along the now well-worn path to the cabin. This was job a usually allotted to me, and one I found boring and soul-destroying. It seemed never ending, even worse than barking timber. The chips were used in the stove to warm the cabin up quickly. Chips crackling and spitting inside the stove, the wood aroma floating about the cabin, and looking forward to a good tea was a most satisfying end to a day as the shades of night settled around us.

Our 10 horsepower Ruston Hornsby. This was the engine I helped to keep steam up in at Rhayader. Under the tree in the background is the cabin. The push bench in the foreground was for sawing firing wood for the engine.

When enough trees had been felled to give a good spell of sawing and to fulfil a number of orders for sawn timber, the next job was to winch the trees down through the wood, a distance of about five hundred yards or so to the edge of a ford through the river. The tractor was then driven across the ford, and used to winch the trunks over, several at a time. It was a grand sight to stand on the river bank high above the water and look down on the trees floating on the surface as they were slowly winched across as the flow of the water tried to sweep them downriver. And so the work went on all day.

When all the timber in the stack had been got across, or enough had been stacked by the rack bench to give a good spell of sawing, it was time to get steam up in the old engine and once again watch Father and Uncle roll a stick on the bench, with the engine doing her stuff as faithfully as ever.

As the cutting depth of the saw above the bench was two foot six inches, during the first cut the trees were too big for the saw to reach right through, so the saw remained buried in the stick for the full eighteen foot length of the cut. It was wonderful to see the old engine working away at it, going hammer and tongs and well up to her work, with the muted sound of the saw as it travelled through the tree, breaking out at the end of the cut as if with a great sigh of relief. Then the beat of the engine fell away to a more restful sound and the urgent rocking to and fro slacked off to a gentle pace. After running the stick back through the saw, screaming and howling as if in protest, the engine was shut off, and the remaining unsawn part of the tree that the saw could not reach was split open. The red beauty of the timber when it was converted

Sawing at Rhayader 1953-4. The saw protruded 2 feet 6 inches above the bench, leaving about 18 inches to split open after the cut had been made. Uncle Idris is standing by the tree.

into various sizes was worth seeing. Due to wartime restrictions all the timber had to be sold to a licensed timber merchant.

Some evenings here in the cabin we might discuss the merits of different kinds of timber, their uses, advantages and disadvantages for various jobs, their weights, hardness, colouring, texture, and country of origin. Here I learnt that it was David Douglas who brought the Douglas Fir tree into this country, and it is named after him. I heard how larch is a very durable timber for fencing, and was warned how chestnut could be made to look like oak, and I was told that a Petrograd Standard equals 165 cubic feet. As the days and evenings passed I learned and absorbed far more than in months of schooling. Yet such a lot of it I have now forgotten as the years roll on and I have no more use for the knowledge that I gained in my early years.

When all was still and quiet with not a breath of wind outside, the cabin was filled with peace and silence as the fire in the stove died down. When there came a lull in the conversation, I would ask, 'Can you hear anything? Can you hear the river running by?'

Father and Uncle would tilt their heads slightly and take on an attitude of listening, then nod slowly with eyes half closed against the white light from the Tilley lamp hissing overhead and from the warmth of the stove and the efforts of the day's labour.

Our cabin under a fir tree on the last sawmilling site near Rhayader. On the right behind the tree is the engine and tack all packed up ready to be moved, but it never was, for it was the end of steam sawing as we knew it. Ten years after this job finished another such job came our way, but Father and Uncle had by then sold all the tack, the Fowler, the Roby, the Burrell and even the cabin.

I marvelled that their hearing was so acute and was sorrowful that I was never going to hear it for myself. I was deprived even of the hissing of the Tilley lamp.

This was the last sawing job where the cabin was used, and when they moved to another job, they left the cabin until the time came to dismantle it. One night in a high wind a great limb of the tree that shaded the cabin crashed down through the roof, leaving the cabin open to the elements, and many things were stolen from it. I had always been afraid that this would happen and would lie awake in my bunk on windy nights as the cabin shuddered in the blast from the wind. I could picture in my mind's eye the great branches of the tree swaying and creaking, ready to break off and fall on the cabin, crushing us to death. I used to ask Father 'Why did you put the cabin by this tree?'

'For shade in summer, David,' he replied. 'It gets very hot and uncomfortable inside if the cabin is out in the sun all day.' I many times tried to persuade him to move it, but to no avail.

The cabin after a huge branch had crashed down through the roof one stormy night.

Several years later, when I had left school and was putting the knowledge that I had learnt from Father and Uncle into practice, Father and I were at home doing some sawing in the shop. Come evening time, having shut the engine off and finished sawing for the day while Father was preparing our evening meal – Mother was away looking after Aunt Ada – I occupied myself turning over the garden in preparation for planting, it being springtime.

Eventually we sat down at the table and enjoyed a good wholesome meal of broth. Sitting at the table feeling replete after our meal, I decided I had better go and do some more gardening. After turning over a few more spits the thoughts of tomorrow's sawing began to weigh heavily on my mind, as the space under the push bench was full of sawdust. I drove my spade into the ground and hurried back into the house to see Father.

'Are we going to do some more sawing tomorrow?' I asked.

'Yes,' he replied, nodding his head.

'I had better go and clear the sawdust out then,' I said, 'or we won't be starting very early. I'll have a drink of water first', I said, moving past him through the door, making my way towards the pantry and a nice long drink of water. As I cleared the sawdust away I broke off every now and again to go back up to the house to have a drink of water. Father would look at me, grin a bit to himself but say nothing.

At tea time next day, a different meal this time, I said to Father, 'Boy, that broth was good, but I drank about a bucket of water afterwards. And I had to get up in the night to have several drinks.'

Father, laughing, said 'You enjoyed it, did you?'

He was very partial to salt and used plenty of it. He could cook anything and did not have a lot of time for those men who had to be waited on hand and foot.

'Salt is good for you,' he used to say, 'it's purifying'. He used to keep a bag of salt in the shed and used it liberally.

One evening Father and I talked about the different places where he had worked and he told me the story of a return from working at Newbridge-on-Wye, a distance of about thirty miles.

'It was with the Roby in summertime. I was driving and we started out about four o'clock and wanted to get home before dark.'

'You must have been getting along,' I said.

'Yes we were shifting, especially down the bank past the Fforest Inn. My, we were shifting down that bank,' said Father, shaking his head and pursing his lips at the memory of it.

'Must have took some keeping on the road I bet,' I said.

'Oh no, old Tom was steering,' replied Father.

'I see,' I said. Old Tom's steermanship was legendary.

Father carried on. 'Yes, there was old Tom steering, myself driving, Papa Price sat on the tool box on the back of the bunker, Uncle on one belly tank, Joe the Vron [who worked for father for a spell] on the other belly tank and Harry hanging on as well.'

'What a sight,' I said, and thought about the engine thundering down the bank, going like the wind in the twilight with six men hanging on all round the engine for dear life. Just picture them all. The Roby in the twilight thundering down the one

Sawing at the Letty not far from Newbridge-on-Wye. Note the old Morris car, the living van beyond the car, the portable engine and the Roby – a great scene from the days of steam.

Another view of sawing at the Letty, giving a clearer view of the living van and the portable engine. The van was a thing of great beauty with a wealth of carvings inside and out, and numerous brass fittings including a brass fender round the stove, which also had a small brass sway over it. One weekend whilst we were at home, the van was broken into and most of the brass fittings were stolen. When this sawing job was finished we moved on to another job, left the van, a wagon and a set of wheels there intending to pick them up another day. But we never did. Father and I went there in the sixties, but there was no sign of the van or wagon.

mile bank from off the top of Radnor Forest with six men hanging on all round the engine. The noise from the gears would be ringing round the hills, the big ends would be just a blurr, the eccentrics and rods would be tumbling and scissoring like bees' wings. The water would be showing well in the glass. The needle on the pressure gauge would be minutely wavering with the vibration from the engine, and the fly wheel spinning round like green fire. On the footplate would have been Father with one hand on the regulator, his other hand on the reverse lever keeping an ever watchful eye over it all. Standing by the side of him would have been Old Tom, one of the greatest steersmen of the day, handling the wheel like a maestro and with his pipe clamped firmly between his teeth and his moustache bristling down over the stem, keeping the engine arrow-straight on the road, taking the curves as if he was glued just the right distance out from the verge. Both of them would have stood with their knees slightly bent so as to lessen the shake from the engine, and all of them grim-faced with their teeth rattling in their heads as they silently urged Father on to ever greater speeds.

'Were you out of gear going down the bank?' I asked.

'No,' he replied, giving me a fierce look. I should have known better than to have asked such a question. He had drummed it into me enough times: 'Never run your engine out of gear.'

'Did you get home before dark?' I asked Father. 'Just about,' he replied.

A line of work that Father undertook towards the end of his working life was well sinking. Father had often explained to me how you line a well with stone,

---

Telegrams:
"SPRUCE, WEDNESBURY"
"SPRUCE, SMETHWICK"
"SPRUCE, WOLVERHAMPTON"
"SPRUCE, STOURPORT-ON-SEVERN"

Telephones:
WEDNESBURY 0521 (8 Lines)
SMETHWICK 1218 (3 Lines)
WOLVERHAMPTON 21475
(4 Lines)
STOURPORT 132 (2 Lines)

C. WALSH GRAHAM LTD

WEDNESBURY

TIMBER IMPORTERS — JOINERY MANUFACTURERS
ROOFING CONTRACTORS — BUILDERS' MERCHANTS
WALLBOARD IMPORTERS — BOX AND CASE MANUFACTURERS

PLEASE QUOTE   OUR REF.   YOUR REF.   DATE
4th February, 1953.

Mr. L. T. Price,
Pernyn,
Brilley,
Whitney-on-Wye,
HEREFORD.

Dear Llew,

Reg Mills will come up to Rhayder first thing on Monday next for the load of 2" x 7" and all being well return again on Tuesday for a load of 1½" T.&T. and if you can manage it a further load of 1½" on Wednesday. We can do with up to 1,000cu.ft. 1½" T.&T. all told.

Yours faithfully,
for C. WALSH GRAHAM LTD.

Managing Director.

An order from C. Walsh Graham for sawn timber, showing how busy they were in getting the orders out.

working from the top down. After deciding on the spot where you were going to sink your well, the spot having been found with the aid of a forked hazel stick, you dug down ten foot. Then you dug into the sides of the well four holes, two one side and two on the opposite side. You made sure to dig in a considerable distance. You then inserted baulks of good sound oak timbers, roughly 12 inches square, into these holes, securely packing and bedding them in. Using these timbers as a base for the stone you then lined the walls of the well up to the mouth. On completing this task you then dug down another ten foot. You then inserted more oak timbers, but at 90 degrees to the ones above. You then lined the well up to the first set of timbers, then dug down another ten foot, again inserting timbers this time in the same directions as the top pair, and lined the well up to the previous pair of timbers. You continued on down the well in this manner until you struck water.

Once when I was helping Father sink a well at one farm out in a nice green sward field, I was on the winder winching up the spoil, Father was at the head of the well emptying the full bucket as it came up from the bottom, whilst Uncle was at the foot of the shaft cutting down into the bowels of the earth.

During the morning's work the sun advanced across the sky and arrived at our dinner hour. I heaved a sigh of relief as Father shouted down to Uncle, 'It's dinner time, you coming up?'

Back up the well shaft floated the hollow reply, 'Yes.'

Father turned towards me and said 'He's coming up,' nodding his head and raising his hand with his thumb uppermost to signify that Uncle was going to ride up in the bucket on this lift, then turning back to watch him settle himself comfortably in the bucket. A shout of 'Alright' from Uncle and 'alright' from Father back down to him, was followed by another shout of 'Alright, wind up' coming back up from Uncle. Father now half turned towards me, so that he was sure I could lip read him, and gave me the signal to start winding. He then turned back to look down the well to make sure that Uncle was coming up safely. I myself watched Father for any sign that he might give me should anything happen. I continued winding. Then Uncle's cap appeared above the rim of the well shaft, the rest of him coming slowly into view. I kept on winding so that he could step onto the safety planks over the mouth of the well. I then turned the handle on the winch a little more until I felt the brake drop into place and stopped winding. This acted as a steady on the rope for him which he was still grasping with one hand. Although the brake was on I still held the handle as an extra safety precaution until I saw him move away some yards from the well. These were all our own safety rules – crude but effective, and they stood us in good stead over the years.

Yet within minutes Uncle was to break one of our rules, and within three-quarters of an hour I was to break one myself. Such is human nature. The outcome could have been serious, but due to how we worked nothing of consequence came amiss.

Once I had completed winding Uncle up, I changed gear ready to let him back down after dinner and engaged the safety arm to stop them jumping out of gear. I always made sure of this very important item after each lift on the winch and at every stop for meals or whatever. But as I moved away to get my grub bag I noticed out of the corner of my eye Uncle go to the winch, do something to it and say something to Father, at the same time lifting the safety arm and letting it drop back. By this time I was making great inroads into my dinner and did not take too much notice of what Uncle was doing or saying to Father. My mind was at rest that I had left the winch with the safety arm engaged, ready for the next start after dinner. Also, I had double-checked it.

While having dinner, I recall mentioning a rock that projected into the shaft and wondered whether we ought to shore it up. But Father reckoned it was quite safe. 'However, I think we should strike water soon as I can hear it running like anything. Can you hear it?' he asked Uncle.

'Yes,' he replied, 'very loud and clear indeed. I thought we would have struck it by now.'

'How deep are we?' I asked, as I basked in the warm sunshine.

'About twenty to twenty-five foot, I would say,' said Uncle.

'We will have to stop before long,' said Father. 'This well is unlined and if it comes on a wet spell it will be too dangerous to carry on working down there at this depth. If we make thirty foot and there is no water we will have to think again. If it starts to rain heavy those sides will start peeling off.'

'Make it thirty foot,' I said 'and if there is no water give it up. Should that rock fall while you're working down there, you will never come out of there alive.'

'Well, we'd best get on,' we agreed amongst ourselves as we squinted at the sun, trying to judge how much it had travelled during our dinner break. 'But let us measure the depth first.'

Getting the measure and letting it down the well, it read twenty-one feet.

'Another ten feet and that's it,' I said.

So, having got ready to make a fresh start, Uncle sits in the bucket, swings out over the well and I gently lower him down, keeping a firm hold on the handle and pushing it in towards the gearing as a precaution should anything go wrong with the safety arm. All of a sudden, when he's about ten foot from the bottom, wheeeee – out flies the rope from the winch, the drum spinning round at a terrific speed, and down the well goes Uncle.

'What the heck is wrong?' I thought to myself looking at the consternation on Father's face as he tried to slow down the rope that was sliding through his hand, but letting it go or he would suffer rope burn. Meanwhile I pushed hard at the handle, trying to mesh the cogs. It was all over in a few seconds. Uncle landed with a bump on the bottom and Father shouted down to him, 'You alright?'

Up comes the reply, 'Yes, but I'm fast in the bucket.' Father and I were peering down the well, watching Uncle's antics as hopped about like a great fat toad wearing a cap, trying to extract his posterior from the bucket.

'Is he alright?' I asked Father.

'Yes,' he replied, 'but he's fast in the bucket.' Uncle was sat in the bucket with his two hands pushing down at its rim. All of a sudden and with one great push he extracted himself. I could almost hear a pop.

'Ah well,' I said to Father, 'if he is alright let him stop down there for a bit. He will be cooled off by the time he comes back up.'

I went back to look at the winch to see what had come amiss. There was the safety arm resting on top of the cog wheel instead of being engaged. 'How the earth did that get there?' I thought. 'I always check that arm.' Father came over to give me a hand to sort the rope out and get everything ship-shape. We then carried on working.

After a couple of hours or so I wound Uncle back up to the surface to change over with Father. 'I would have kicked your backside, if I could have got at you,' he said.

'Look, you shouldn't have been messing about with my winch at dinner time. I recall you left the safety arm on top of the cogs instead of engaging it.'

'You should have seen to that,' replied Uncle.

'I do, I do, after each wind up,' I said. 'You mucked it up at dinner time.'

The rule that Uncle had broken was: Never mess about with another man's machine. If for some reason you have to, leave everything as you found it. He left the safety arm out of engagement. The one I broke was: Although you have checked and double-checked your machine previously, check it again just before you use it after being absent from it. I failed to check it after our meal break. Well, we ended up alright about it.

After a few days, having got down thirty-one feet and with still no sign of water, although it could be heard running very loud and clear, the weather started to take a turn for the worse. It was no longer safe to work down the well, so the boards were put over the opening and made secure. We tied the fence up round the site and made our way off down the fields towards home.

Next morning it was still raining, so we went to another job. The heavy rain continued for several days. After a week or so, when we had finished the job in hand and the rain had ceased, and the ground had dried up a bit, we decided to do some more work down at the well. Arriving at the well head and removing the boards covering the mouth of the well, peering down the shaft we could see that quite a lot of peeling of the sides had taken place and there was a large quantity of it down at the bottom.

'That's a lot of stuff to remove,' I said.

'Yes that's what too much rain will do to an unlined well. I knew it could happen, but I didn't think it would have been quite as bad as this', said Father. 'It was very

Top: Myself and the second Nil Desperandum. In the mid 1950s my Father had had to scrap the Fowler, but we transferred its nameplate to our new engine. Father and I are about to set off from the other side of Craven Arms for home, a distance of around 40 miles, in the early 1960s. (We would first have to remove the brick from the top of the safety valve cover at the top of the chimney.) Compare this with the lower photo of some 50 years earlier which shows Maurice Price standing by the smoke box of his Burrell, and his grandson Sid by the belly tank, a photo I think taken at Craven Arms station where they were hauling timber. Maurice bought the tractor brand new in 1913 for £500 and paid for it within 12 months.

heavy rain though. However, we'll put some iron bands down and seal the sides with some round stuff out of the wood. I'll go down then and have a look what it's like.'

So we got busy lowering the iron bands down and driving timbers in behind them. Then a fresh start was made to remove the fallen debris. This was very wet and heavy and proved hard work indeed to remove. Father's and Uncle's feet were sinking down into the ooze, making any kind of movement extremely difficult. After each spell down at the bottom they were coming up in a terrible mess, their clothes plastered in mud and soaking wet.

After a while we could examine the walls of the well and it was decided that it was no longer safe or feasible to continue, and a decision was made to abandon the work. We put the boards back over the well mouth, loaded our tack onto the trailer, tied the fence up and made our way down the fields.

The well was later filled in with the spoil that we dug out. Because we had failed, no money was asked for and no offer was made to us. That's working for yourself.

According to the water diviner we should have found water at fifteen foot, which would have been over our usual maximum safe depth. We went well beyond this depth. Usually we only went ten foot deep in an unlined well. On reaching ten foot we then lined the well out.

On sinking another well, rock was struck at fifteen foot and was proving very slow going, blasting all the time. So it was abandoned and a new well was sunk about three hundred yards further down the field. This was successful.

A well had been sunk at Cooper's Cottage some time before the Old Man's time, possibly by his father or grandfather. It is reputed to be over eighty feet deep and is lined out with stone. However, when the well was sunk initially, the work stopped at eighty feet down as solid rock was hit with still no sign of water. So the well was abandoned, and over the years succeeding generations threw all manner of rubbish down it.

Instead, drinking water for the cottage had to be obtained from one of four possible sources, but usually from the well at Pentrejack, a mile down the lane.

When I asked Father who used to carry all the water from Pentrejack to keep the cottage supplied, he replied 'Anybody that was available.'

I also enquired, 'Did you have a yoke?'

'No,' he said, 'but we did have a square frame which we walked inside and this frame held the buckets out from your body very steady and stopped the water spilling while you walked.'

As this was a very time-consuming and laborious means of obtaining your daily supply, one day Father decided to clean the well out and see what he could do to obtain water. This entailed much work as the well was very nearly full of rubbish, and it was a big day when once again that self-same rock that stopped previous generations all those years ago was uncovered.

Papa Price and Uncle were now helping Father and after making an examination of the rock they decided to go ahead and blast it. So they bored a hole in the rock to receive a charge of blasting powder, tamped it well home and lit the fuse, followed by a hurried scoot up the ladder and over the top before the charge went off. The old cottage trembled and shook on its foundations when the blast occurred, and the crocks and china rattled on the Welsh dresser.

After blasting operations you couldn't go down the well for a fortnight, due to the smoke and fumes. Once this had cleared a candle was lowered down, but there was no sign of any water and a layer of rock was still visible. So a second charge was prepared and the fuse lit, with the fuse lighter scurrying up the ladder. When another fortnight had passed, the rock was again examined but with no better results. So it was decided to use a bigger charge.

This blast shook the old cottage even more, the china rattled on the dresser and one roof sheet of the shed over the well head went heavenwards. After the usual fortnight had passed they prepared to go down the well to clear the spoil, but lo and behold, there was ten foot of water in the bottom of the well. They had succeeded in cracking the rock and letting the water into the well and from that day forward it never went dry and they were never again short of water. It was a day of rejoicing for the family, as a good well freed them from the everlasting chore of fetching and carrying water. Also, where we once went to people for water, now in dry spells they came to us.

When we were carrying out some repairs to the pump which was down the well, Father said to me 'Go down and put these bolts in. At the same time make sure you look at the timbers that I told you about.'

So taking the spanner and bolts off him I stepped out over the well mouth onto the ladder peering down, down into the blackness, 70 foot and 10 foot of water made 80 foot below me. It was like stepping out into space. Anyhow, I descended the ladder into the well, reached the pump and put in the bolts as asked, then I took a good look around me. The timbers were black, wet and looked as if they were charred. I looked at the terrific amount of stone that it took to line the well shaft out. It all had to be lowered down the well in a bucket and woe betide you

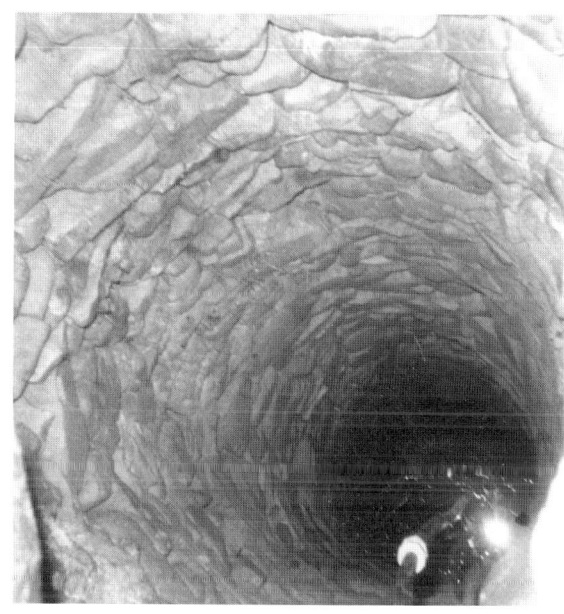

Looking down the well at Pentrejack.

if a stone fell out on the way down for there would be a man working down below. Also the baulks of oak timber of that size were no light weight to handle. It was an altogether laborious job: the digging and winding up and carting away of the spoil, lowering timbers and stone down the well, including finding and carting stone to the well head. I wondered which of my grandfathers had sunk this well. The stone and everything was dripping wet, with the water droplets dripping everywhere, including all over myself. Father very often used to come up out of the well soaking wet and very cold. He used to wear an old leather coat and cap and brown sacking to help to keep him dry.

Looking about and thinking about these things, my gaze travelled round and up the stonework. Leaning back and keeping a firm grip on the vertical ladder, I raised my eyes to the well mouth, trying at the same time not to get water droplets in my eyes that were coming down like great drops of rain, peering up through them at the well mouth. Heck, good night alive, tighten my grip on the ladder, for the hole at the top had grown smaller, with the sides of the well closing in on me and a funny-looking round thing peering down at me, which was Father's face. It looked like a head with no body resting on the edge of the well mouth. Realising that it was only an illusion, I've had enough of this, I thought to myself, I'm getting up out of here. Taking a last look at the pump I quickly climbed up the ladder, feeling better as I neared the top, the daylight growing stronger and looking better all the time. As I regained the top and stepped onto terra firma, Father was looking intently at me and smiling away.

Perhaps I looked a bit wan. But I can assure you, if you don't like heights you won't like depths. Down a well, not only have you got depths, above you, but below you you've got heights as you peer down into the inky black waters below that are always alive, rippling from the water droplets splashing down.

Father often used to say that when they were working down the well, if it rained heavy it took about a week for the rainwater to reach the bottom. You could see the damp advancing slowly down the stonework, so many yards each day, and different shades of damp for different rainy days.

Once mains water came into the area and was laid on, the well was never used again. The water became polluted by creosote seeping in from a nearby electricity pole. This destroyed a good supply of water. One member of our family even attributed healing properties to it and used to come for a supply to drink and rub on his legs, though what his complaint was I never knew. After we sold the cottage, the new owners filled the well in.

One of the other jobs that we used to do was to carry out repairs to a wind pump belonging to Holborn Farm. It was used to raise the water up out of a 212 foot deep bore hole and pump it some 300 yards or so up to a reservoir for supplying the farm with water.

Sometimes a wooden pump rod would break or there would be trouble with the foot valves being silted up. When the trouble was due to silting, we used to take so much off the bottom of the pipe. Eventually this led to the pipe being above the now silted up water supply and the abandonment of the bore hole. However, when it was a broken pump rod, we of course made and fitted a new one. This entailed fitting our pulley blocks above the bore hole, rising the rods until the broken rod was located which confirmed the trouble. Being that the rods travelled up and down inside the water supply pipe (when working), this meant that we then had to rise the piping with the pulley blocks to get at the broken rod and to make and bolt a new one in place, then lower it all back down the bore hole. It wasn't a bad job on a nice warm summer's day, but when it was wet, cold and windy, it was far from pleasant.

One night of a high wind the mill wheel came off the spindle. When it hit the ground it bent the framing and sails very badly. The key holding the wheel on had worked loose and fallen out, which was the reason for the wheel coming off, so having cut a new key (the old one was never found), dismantled the mill wheel and sails and straightened it all out on the anvil, we proceeded to put it all back on the spindle which was at the top of the tower approximately 25 feet above the ground, Having re-fitted the hub we started bolting on the sails.

It was a perfect morning to start the job, not a breath of wind, so Uncle and I set to bolting it all together, with myself scurrying up and down the tower ladder, passing the sails up when required and bolting up the outer rim, at the same time tying the bolted section to the tower frame with a piece of cord in case the wind came up and started to turn the incomplete wheel. Uncle was stood on the little platform bolting the sails onto the hub. Having got half the sails on, all of a sudden up sprang the wind just before I could retie the half-completed wheel and round went the wheel lumping round all out of balance. Without hesitation I nipped back down the ladder and picked up a stake which was lying on the ground. Looking back up at Uncle stood on the little platform behind the wheel I hurried back up the ladder, ready to jam the stake in the wheel in case there was any danger to him. However I then realized I could not use it as it would swing the tail round bringing the sails out of the wind, knocking Uncle off the platform. There was Uncle stood on a little two foot platform which had no guard rails, looking as cool as a cucumber with the wheel lumping round in front of him and no means of stopping it. At any moment the whole lot could swing round as the tail came into play, keeping the wheel into the face of the wind and sweeping Uncle off his perch. If that happened I hoped to goodness he would grab the tail and go round with it out of harm's way. But at that very moment the wind dropped off completely and the wheel came to a stop.

Glancing down to make sure nobody was underneath, I dropped the stake, ran up the last few rungs of the ladder and securely tied the wheel. We then carried on bolting on the sails, turning the wheel round in order to bolt the next one on, tying it to the tower after each turn. So we continued on like this until we had completed the job, giving the key a final blow or two with the hammer to make sure it was tight.

When we had finished and had descended back down to the ground, we both stood back looking up at the now completed wheel becalmed with not a breath of wind to turn it. Uncle said to me 'We want some wind now.'

'Aye,' I replied, 'what was it like up on the perch when the wind came up and started turning the wheel?'

'Alright,' he said looking at me with a grin.

Some years later on the wheel again came off. We put it on once more even though it was by now getting a bit bent about. Later on it was abandoned due to the bore hole silting up. Only the tower now remains, with the little wooden platform where Uncle once stood over thirty years ago.

As the years went by Father and Mother used to remark when we were having tea with the windows wide open on a warm summer's evening, 'We don't hear the windmill creaking now.' I never ever heard it myself.

One of the other many and various jobs that they used to carry out was hauling lime out from the kilns to the surrounding farms ready for spreading on the land. This was not the nice white hydrated lime that you obtain in bags from builders' merchants today. This was quicklime, or burnt or lumplime as I've heard it called. From what I can remember, it always appeared a dirty yellow-white colour and had to be protected from moisture during transit otherwise it would rapidly heat up. Father had at least one wagon-load of lime smoking away behind the engine as he hauled it along. It has been known for lime to burn a wagon out completely. It was also unpleasant to handle due to the burns it could cause. Near one of the kilns was some ground grazed by donkeys, one of which fell into the kiln. As the heat in the kiln was terrific, it must have been a terrible end for the poor donkey.

Hauling two wagon-loads of lime from the Old Radnor limekilns up to Hundred House. It was uphill virtually all the way to Fforest Inn where they took on water. The Fowler would be working hard and Father said you had to be a real engine driver to be able to keep the big end cool whilst still firing up to keep steam up. Coming back light was easier and the engine would thunder up the Old Radnor pitch throwing sparks high into the sky at 2 o'clock in the morning. It was a long journey.

4 Stories round the fire

Often of an evening in the bungalow, Father would poke the fire up in the old Yorkist Cooking Range as we basked in the warmth given out by the glowing coals on dark winter evenings. Some slack at the back of the fire would sliding down onto the red embers in the front, flaring up and showing the smoke rising up the back of the chimney. Having made up the fire to his satisfaction and hanging the poker that he had made on the damper handle, he would lean back in his armchair and looking me in the eye would start his stories.

Father told me that once the Old Man had gone down to Hereford one morning on the train, having got on the train at Whitney Station. He wanted to buy some iron rods of about $\frac{1}{4}$ inch to $\frac{3}{8}$ inch diameter. Having purchased the rods and made a bundle, he heaved the bundle up on his shoulder and walked through Hereford back to the station. Finding that the bundle of rods was too long to go in the goods van, he pulled some binder twine out of his pocket and tied them on to the running board step on the outside of the railway carriage. Having made all secure he climbed into the carriage and sat down ready and waiting to head for Whitney. Arriving at Whitney Station and alighting from the carriage, he untied his bundle of rods, hoisted them on his shoulder and made his way up the road home to Pentrejack. And nobody said one word to him. He looked a character who was not to be trifled with, with his great white beard and a horse-hair cider mat over his shoulders to keep the wet out.

'People were more out to help you in those days,' said Father as he paused in his narrative to poke the fire up, 'and I don't suppose it could be done today.'

'The Old Man was threshing down at Pentrejack,' continued Father. 'Which farm he was threshing at I don't know. But on this farm was a lady, whether she was a lady farmer or the farmer's wife again I don't know, as it was before my time and a good many years ago. Anyway, the lady used to like to keep an eye on things and see for herself what was going on. One of the things that she was very fond of doing when all the men were out of the way having their dinner in the house, was to go up the ladder on to the top of the drum. What for no one ever knew. On this occasion she slipped out of the house and climbed up the ladder onto the top of the drum

This roller belonged to Mr. Chambers of Clifford and was driven by Bill Lewis. The accident happened in 1912 not far from the Red Lion inn in Bredwardine. My father and Papa Price went to have a look and discover what had caused it. Apparently Bill missed getting the roller into gear when changing at the top of the bank, and the roller ran away downhill. Bill decided he would try and go through a gateway into a field instead of trying to take the bend in the road, but after crashing through the gate he discovered a deep ditch. Unfortunately Bryan Webb, who was riding on the draw bar, got crushed between the roller and the living van that the roller was pulling.
The moral of the story was: Never change gear without first squatting your engine (putting a block of timber under a wheel on the downhill side)

safely. But on the way back down disaster struck. Her feet slipped on the ladder rungs and she fell through and got wedged in a very undignified position, with her long skirt and clothes way up above her waist, and with no amount of struggling could she free herself. Finding herself in such a jam, there was nothing for it but to shout for help, which brought the men all out of the house to free her. This put paid to her little trips up to the top of the drum at dinnertime.'

He sat there for some time listening intently, then saying 'It's raining and pouring outside and the wind's rising,' he reached over for the Good Book to do some reading. So I buried myself in John Bourne's *A Catechism of the Steam Engine* as I read the evening away.

On another evening Father mentioned he was once working on a smallholding which was owned by two old bachelors, carrying out some minor repairs to the house such as re-pegging a few stone tiles that had slipped, some pointing to the chimney and so on. Relating the story to me some years afterwards, he said what a beautiful old black and white house it was.

'Come dinner time one of the bachelors said "Bring your sandwiches in the house, Mr. Price. We will make you a cup of tea."' So Father picked up his frail (his food bag, which he very often called a frail), washed his hands under the pump and made his way into the house where they all sat down at a long deal-boarded table. Underneath the tabletop was a drawer for keeping knives and forks in directly over which was a small hole in the tabletop. As the meal proceeded – the two bachelors' meal consisted of bread and cheese – the crumbs from the bread got scattered over the table and a mouse came out of the hole, ran across the table, picked up a bread-crumb in its mouth, ran back across the table and popped back down the hole.

This steam cart with slab shod wheels also belonged to Mr. Chambers of Clifford, the driver again being Bill Lewis. The cart would hold 5 tons. Papa Price at one time worked for Mr. Chambers. On one occasion he ran from the top of Huntington some 3.5 miles downhill to Mahollam, near Kington, out of gear – heaven knows what speed he reached. In 1908 he borrowed the steam cart and living van to move back to Brilley from Ewyas Harold, where he had been residing when in charge of the portable engine driving the sawmill at Pontrilas, to live at the Cooper's Cottage and help the Old Man, his father, with the threshing. En route they stopped near Moccas to brew up and Aunty Ciss went to a nearby house to ask for some water to make some tea, whereupon she was asked if she always went about like this.

A Man steam cart belonging to Mr. Chambers of Clifford. Maurice Price is the driver, and Bill Lewis on the right. This was perhaps taken at Clifford Station, due to the presence of the unknown man in the railway uniform. Below, another of Mr. Chambers' carts.

One of the bachelors looked at Father and said 'By cum he's a sharp un,' and they all carried on with their meal with no more comment about the mouse, said Father.

We were both laughing at the novelty of it. 'Did they open the drawer to try and catch the mouse?' I asked. 'No,' he replied. 'No attempt was made to do anything.'

Some years later I worked for the same people, now more advanced in years. I sat at the same table where Father sat to eat my sandwiches and I saw the same hole in the tabletop but no mouse this time. They were good and nice people to work for and I used to like working for them. Well they are all dead and gone now and the mouse too, I suppose.

Looking hard at me to see if I realized that he had changed the subject, but with such a piercing look that I wondered what was coming, I struggled to adjust my lip-reading to a different run of words. Giving Father a nod to signify that I understood and adjusting my features to correspond, he relaxed his look, and leaning forward in his armchair he started off again.

'The Old Man, great-grandfather, was walking to or from his day's threshing across the fields by way of a footpath. Suddenly, some distance from him, he saw a horde of rats on the move, led by a white rat. He did not go anywhere near them, but kept well out of their way and hurried on along the path to get away from them. If you got in the way of a swarm that size or tried to stop them they would most likely swarm all over you.'

'Where did the white rat come from?' I asked.

Shutting his eyes and shaking his head from side to side, 'I don't know,' he replied, 'I am only repeating what the Old Man told me.'

Still with his eyes closed and opening the palms of his hands towards the warmth of the fire he continued. 'At the Cefn there used to be a piece of ground that was fair heaving with rats. The place was overrun with them yet the farmer would not kill any of them or allow anyone else to do so.' Opening his eyes to see if I was following, he carried on. 'However, he had a boy working for him, and one day the boy killed a rat. The farmer saw him do it and told him off about it saying, "That rat has got as much right to live as what you have."

'At one time some carpenters were carrying out some work there during a very warm spell of weather. The farmer had a barrel of cider in the shed from which he told the carpenters that they could quench their thirst. They were to go in the shed and help themselves. So every now and again they would go in the shed and have a drink. These carpenters used to push-bike up from Kington to their day's work and back at night. Eventually they finished the job and departed.

'After twelve months had elapsed they were once again back at the farm to do some more work. The cider barrel was now empty and the farmer decided to clean it out. When he broke into the barrel, out tumbled some rat skeletons. The farmer took the carpenters round to the barrel to show them what he had found and one man was apparently sick on the spot.'

Both Mother and I were turning our nose up at the thought of it, saying, 'Ugh that's terrible.'

'Well, at lots of places they used to use water out of the pool to put in the cider barrel, and just the other side of the pool the cows would be stood in the water drinking. The apples would be kept in the orchard under the trees, with the chickens walking and pecking all over them. Nobody seemed to get bad from it – different today.'

One of the stories that my father had been told himself concerned some geese. The farming folk at a particular farm had been making cider. What was left of the apples after going through the mill and press was very often thrown out in the orchard and it has been known for the pig on the farm to gain access to this apple pulp, make a meal of it and become drunk. But unbeknown to the farming folk, the geese made a meal of it and when they came upon them every one of them had keeled over and passed out. They thought that they were all dead (perhaps there was hardly a breath of life in them). But the geese could not be wasted and so they promptly feathered them. Sometime later the geese began to revive – I don't know who was the most surprised, the folk or the geese. It must have been cold and painful to wake up with no feathers on and every one plucked out. I bet they had goose-pimples alright. As it was too early to prepare the geese for Christmas they decided to keep them a bit longer, there being no deep-freezer about in those days. So the folk made a little coat for each goose out of some sacking to help to keep them warm. It must have been a funny sight indeed.

On more than one occasion Father told me about a dog that used to be about Kington Market that used to work for itself as a drover, freelance as you might say. When a neighbour farmer of ours bought some cattle or sheep at the market, this dog used to help him to drive the stock home to his farm, a distance of five miles. Having completed this task and seen the stock safely in the yard, the farmer would give the dog a meal and a drink as a reward. Thus sustained, the dog would make its way out of the yard down the lane back to Kington Market for some more work. What became of the dog in the end I never found out. Father did not know who was the owner of the dog or if it lived about the market by itself or even if it had a home to go to; neither did the farmer know.

One evening I asked Father about a postman's hut which I'd heard had once existed somewhere in the area

'There used to be one along the Apostles Lane [a lane that leads north-west from near the top of the hill] in the field belonging to Penlan Farm, just inside the gateway. It was either round or octagon-shaped as you might say, I'm not sure which. The postman's round was a walking round in those days, but even so we used to have our letters at seven or eight o'clock in the morning. When the postman had completed delivering the letters, he didn't return to the post office, but waited in his hut until it was time to make the next collection. Only having completed this duty did he then make his way back to the post office.'

'It must have been a boring spell, waiting all that time' I said.

'Oh I don't know,' replied Father. 'They had it quite comfortable in the hut. They had a stove for warmth and a chair to sit on. They used to make a cup of tea for themselves and filled their time up cobbling boots. So I don't suppose it was too bad.'

I could see that there was more to come. Settling myself deeper in the armchair, stretching my legs out towards the fire, feeling comfortably replete after our evening meal and well satisfied with a good day's work and the old body just starting to ache from the effects of it, I blinked my eyes to lubricate the orbs, as 'tis tiring work lipreading.

Uncle Idris was also a source of stories. He once told me of a time he almost lost control of the Burrell. He and Papa Price were moving the tack from Bailey Maerdy near Whitney-on-Wye to Cabalva to the east of Clyro and had to descend the notoriously steep road down to the Rhydspence. At the top of the pitch he brought the tack to a stop in order to uncouple the wagon and straw tyer so as to take these on a second trip, so lightening the load. Papa got off and walked on ahead to warn anyone coming up what was coming down. Once Uncle Idris was ready, he nudged the regulator open and once underway, wound the brakes on and eased off the regulator. However, the back wheels locked and the Burrell and the drum gathered pace. (The shoes on the Burrell were very hard as they were sent to Germany to be specially hardened. This increased the chance of the wheels locking, and we reshod the Burrell with softer shoes which gave a better grip.) Uncle quickly unwound the brake wheel, opened the regulator to get the back wheels turning so as to get a degree of grip on the road, for on the slide she could have gone anywhere. By now the engine and drum were galloping along at a terrific rate and Uncle wrapped his body around the steering wheel to stop it being whipped out of his hands as one slight diversion from the road and they would be over the edge of a steep drop; he could not afford to take one hand off the wheel to try and slow the engine with the fly wheel brake.

He soon passed Grandad, but he never saw him for the big ends were just a blur. He somehow managed to miss a house that jutted out into the lane, and as the slope eased off he was able to get the engine under control and stop it at the Rhydspence, where he went in for a pint.

'One day,' he continued, 'somebody complained that they were getting their letters too late or something like that. So an Inspector was sent out to investigate and he walked with the postman on his round. When the postman walked the round by himself he knew all the footpaths and shortcuts and used them. But that day with the Inspector he went the long way round by way of the roads which made the round much longer. The outcome was that the Inspector told those who had complained, 'You're lucky to have any post at all up on Brilley Mountain.' Father's face was wreathed in smiles.

'Have you had a cup of tea in the postman's hut?'

'Oh yes,' he replied.

The mention of Apostle's Lane reminded him of another story. 'One day,' he said 'I was coming home along Apostles Lane with the Fowler and an over long train of tack on behind, the drum, living-van, two wagons and boulter. All of a sudden, galloping round the corner and up the road comes the Hunt. The captain's horse on coming face to face with old Nil Desperandum, rears up in the air., and down over the horse's tail slides the captain right into a puddle.'

'"You great thing," he shouted up at the engine and me. "You shouldn't be allowed on the road."

'"I have as much right on the road as you have," I replied, peering down at him from the footplate, hardly able to contain my mirth at the spectacle of the huntsman sat on his backside in a big puddle of water.'

Years later, when they were both somewhat advanced in years, the captain stopped his car outside our gate and Father went to talk to him with no sign of animosity between them on account of the incident that happened many years ago.

Some years after meeting the Hunt along Apostles Lane, Father was up on the roof at Holborn Farm carrying out some repairs. All of a sudden along comes the Hunt galloping up the lane, through the farmyard and through the gate into Kintley field, galloping on down to Kintley Barn.

A little while later into the yard gallops a lone huntsman. 'Have you seen the hounds, what's the best way to go?' he shouts up to Father.

Father, looking up from his work, replies, 'Best way back home I should think.'

Another of his tales involved a donkey. 'There used to be a pub called The New Inn on the pitch on Brilley Mountain where one night many years ago old Mr. Gib was inside drinking his beer. He was a heavy drinker and used to be the owner of a donkey and cart. Some boys passing by the pub and seeing the donkey and cart tied up, took the bit out of the donkey's mouth, twisted it round and put it back in again. So now if you pulled the rein to go left, the donkey felt the pull to the right. Later on that night out of the pub comes Mr. Gib somewhat the worse for drink, unhitches the donkey, leads it on to the road, climbs on to the cart and lets it make its own way along the road. Eventually he wanted to turn off onto a lane, so giving a tug on the rein, the donkey responds in the opposite direction, and the more he pulled on the rein the more the donkey responded, ending up in the hedge. There was old Mr. Gib tugging and shouting "Come on, what's the matter with you?"'

One story that my father told me related to the War Ags, the

Moving railway carriages for Mr. Rothwell in 1928. These carriages were moved using the Roby and a timber carriage from Whitney-on-Wye station to a site about halfway up the Wyeside pitch for use as a dwelling house, where the bungalow Rhydacre is now. Just after making the sharp turn off the main road onto the Wyeside pitch they met the Herefordshire County Council surveyor who commented on the legal width of loads transported by road. My uncle Bill Whittal, who was working with Father that day, outs his 2 foot rule and proceeds to measure the width, taking big jumps every time he stepped the ruler, and lo and behold it came just within the limits. 'Ah well, I suppose so,' said the surveyor. Once the carriages were in place, Father then thatched the roofs so as to keep them cool in summer and warm in winter, and then installed a back boiler for hot water, being paid 1 shilling an hour. However, the lime in the water was so great that the pipes furred up within 12 months. Each day that Father finished his work thatching or plumbing, Mr. Rothwell would pass on his copy of the Daily Worker *newspaper, but Father never read it.*

County War Agricultural Committees which the government set up during the last war. Their job was to make farmers produce more food from their land.

According to my father, one of these War Ag men turned up in a farmer's yard one day wanting to inspect the farm. The farmer replied, 'No you can't come over my farm.'

So the War Ag man pulled a piece of paper out of his pocket and showed it to the farmer saying 'You see this piece of paper?'

'Yes,' replied the farmer.

'Well, this piece of paper gives me the authority to go anywhere I like on your farm.'

The farmer, knowing it was futile to argue, said 'alright'.

So the War Ag man took himself off to view the farm. Sometime later the farmer saw the War Ag man in full flight, running for his life being chased by the bull, whereupon the farmer shouted out to him 'Show him your authority.'

Whether this is a true story or not I don't know.

Father started laughing to himself one evening. 'Your uncle was getting ready to thresh on this farm one morning when the farmer arrived all dressed up in breeches and leggings, looking very smart indeed. He was ready to go to market and was waiting for someone to come and take the cattle for him. All of a sudden the cattle bolted over to the other side of the yard which was knee-deep in sloppy muck. The farmer, not wanting to get himself dirty, especially his highly glossed leggings said to Uncle, "Oh, Mr. Price, could you just slip round the other side of those cattle and drive them back please?"

'Uncle, taking a good look at the cattle and the knee-deep muck he would have to wade through and not liking what he saw, replied, "They're your cattle and it's your muck. You go and get them yourself."

'So there was the farmer in his nice clean breeches and shiny leggings wading through the muck, which he had to clean off the best he could, before going on his way to market in his now much besmeared leggings.'

Looking at me again to assure himself that I'd noticed he was starting a new story, he began, 'There was a concert once taking place in Painscastle and the hall was full of people. Somewhere towards the front of the hall was a man sitting in the audience who had a thick ring of hair just above his ears reaching right round his head, the top of which was completely bald. Every now and again as the concert proceeded he would give this ring of hair a good scratch. This went on for some time until someone at the back of the audience shouted out to him, 'Drive the flea out in the open, you'll catch him easier like that.'

As the embers in the fire died down and the ticking of the clock on the wall and its chiming spoke the lateness of the hour, Father and Mother both drew a long deep sigh and lapsed into silence for a little while. I can picture them now, gazing into the dying embers of the fire as their minds were no doubt thinking of the days gone by, of the people they knew who had departed this life. But the story of the fleas had reminded me of one of my own. While I was staying with my mother's parents at Rhosgoch I went to play in a chicken coop with another little fellow, playing engine drivers, bus drivers and so on. After spending all morning in this wonderful world of make believe, we arranged to play some more after dinner, but my playmate did not turn up, so I spent most of the afternoon in another coop by myself.

I was that young that I was still sleeping with Mother and that night, as I warmed up in bed I started scratching away non stop. Mother threw back the bed clothes and let out a shout, saying 'The boy's covered in fleas, you've been in that coop again. Don't you go in there any more.'

The commotion brought my grandmother into the bedroom to see what all the noise was about. I had to have a real good swill down and a change of bed clothes, the lot. Thank goodness they were chicken fleas. They don't stop on you long, but it was bad enough.

Some evenings we would fall into silence until one of us started telling anything that came to mind. Father once said, 'There were two fellows going down a very steep bank on their push-bikes. The one having failed to take a corner in the road, was thrown off his bike up over a very high hedge. His mate who had managed to come to a stop, having lost sight of him shouted out "You alright?" Back came the reply "I don't know, I haven't landed yet."'

'Is that true?' asked Mother, looking up from a book she was reading.

'I don't know,' replied Father.

'Ah well,' said Mother, 'what goes round and round the room and hides behind the door?' After pondering this for a while I could give no satisfactory answer. 'The broom,' she said, shutting her book.

I remember a conversation with my father after one particularly cold and awful day in which an east wind cut through us all day long. It was now a bitter cold dark winter evening. The fire was roaring in the grate of the cooking range, casting a nice warm glow round the kitchen but fighting a hard battle to keep the bitter cold at bay.

I had just swilled my hands in the bathroom and on coming into the kitchen and sitting down at the table where Father and Mother were already sat eating their tea I said 'Gosh, it's cold out there,' meaning the bathroom which had no heating in those days, 'the water was none too warm,' blowing on my hands and rubbing them together to lend strength to my words.

Father cast a somewhat scornful glance at me over the top of his cup of tea, and lowered it just enough for me to lip read him saying, 'It's a lot better than washing outside in cold water.' After taking another drink and putting his cup back down on its saucer, he looked at me and said, 'When I was going round threshing, we always washed outside under the pump. I've known many times when I've had to break the ice on the water in the hand bowl to get a wash in the mornings.'

Father paused to lower the tea in his cup. Taking advantage of this lull I looked down at my plate and grabbed a few mouthfuls to eat, then took draw on my now cooling cup of tea, at the same time keeping a wary eye on Father in case he should begin once more. It is very difficult to lip read and eat your meal at the same time. When I sat down at the table I used to familiarize myself where everything was with one quick glance but promptly forgot where half of it was. When Father was speaking to me, I slid my left hand along the sandwich on my plate to find the middle of it, at the same time sliding the knife in my right hand along until it came to stop against my left index finger, whereupon I cut the sandwich through. Feeling the side of my plate I tucked the knife under the edge of the plate where I could find it again without looking. Picking up the now smaller portion of my sandwich, I rose it to my mouth, never once taking my eyes off Father's lips.

Father drained his cup, replaced it in its saucer, and continued with his narrative. 'At another farm where I used to thresh, when we stopped for dinner, we were all gathered round the pump trough to wash, the well itself being directly underfoot. The area round the pump and trough was slightly hollow and any spilt water therefore sloshed about underfoot about an inch or so deep. Being that the well was overfull, the water came up between the joints in the flagstones, and with all the men splashing about and washing off the grime and dust from the morning's threshing, the soapy water used to overflow from the trough and mingle with the well water underfoot. So when you pumped a bucket of water up, the soapy water level used to go down.'

'Did the water or tea ever taste soapy?' I asked.

'No,' he replied. 'At least the water was pumped up from the bottom of the well, and the soap would be floating about on the top. But I don't know about dry weather when the water level dropped.'

But Father wasn't the only source of stories. One day while having a break on a job at Glascwm, Uncle said to me, 'At one farm where we used to thresh, just inside the back door in the kitchen was a gravestone.'

Noting the upward tilt of his eyebrows and the slight smile on his face, 'Go on,' I said, 'you're pulling my leg.'

'No I'm not' he replied, shaking his head and his features taking on a serious look.

I was very much astounded and wanted to hear more, so asked 'Was it a flagstone floor and this gravestone was laid amongst them?'

'Yes, that's right,' said Uncle, giving me a nod.

'And did you read what it said?'

'Yes,' he replied, with another nod of his head.

'Well, what did it say then?'

'I don't know now, I don't now remember. It was a long time ago.'

'Was there anyone buried there?'

'Yes, yes,' said Uncle.

'And where was this?' I asked.

There followed a long and detailed explanation as to its whereabouts, but it was too long and detailed for me to lip-read. Many was the time I meant to ask Uncle again the location of this farm, but I never got round to it. Once, on asking Father about it, he replied 'I have heard your Uncle talk about it.'

'Have you seen it yourself?' I asked.

'I don't remember seeing it,' he replied. But next morning, before starting our day's work, Uncle told Father where it was. Father took it all in and with a jerk of his head said not a word.

One evening some sixty years after Uncle had seen this stone, and nearly thirty years after he had died, I was in the shop when a tall farmer appeared and explained that he had brought his mother to see my father. Father was now 91 years old.

There followed talks of old times which we all enjoyed, and so it came about that I was invited to do some work for this man. One day not long afterwards I went to visit the farmer in order to view the work that he wished me to carry out. On entering the farmhouse kitchen, there on the floor right by the back door was the gravestone, just as Uncle said it was. I thought that at last I had discovered the house with the gravestone where Father and Uncle used to thresh all those years ago.

And so I worked at the same place. The house was now empty as the farmer's uncle who lived here had recently died. The farmer said to me one day when we were standing at the head of the large kitchen table, 'Can you see all the men sat round the table at their dinner on threshing day?'

Feeling the hard cold flagstones under my feet and conscious of the beams overhead, I peered down the long table in the dim light from the single window, to the old black cooking range with the mantelpiece above it, as nothing had been altered in this kitchen. I half closed my eyes. I could see Father, Uncle, Harry and all the men; the table laid with steaming victuals and the fire glowing in the grate, with the kettle and pot on the sway keeping warm, and the men talking and bantering as they tucked in, and in the background the womenfolk presiding over all the cooking. 'Yes, yes, I can see them,' I replied.

He looked at me and grinned. I smiled back.

Twelve months later Father died.

But I still don't know why this gravestone was laid in the house.

On another job Uncle and I stopped to have a blow and leaned on our shovels. Turning towards me he said 'You know that bridge over the brook up above Newchurch just by Meredith the Fualt?'

'Yes,' I replied, wondering what was coming.

'Well, I delivered a girder to that bridge when it was being repaired.'

'Where did you get the girder from?' I asked.

'Whitney station,' he replied. 'It came by rail to the station,' he continued, his eyes taking on a faraway look as he recalled the event, 'and I had the job of taking it up to the bridge. So I set out one morning, just myself and the Burrell with the small wagon, a bit too small really, but the timber carriage was in the station yard down at Kington and the ten ton wagon was out on another job. When I got to the station yard, the girder was lying on the ground. Drawing the engine and wagon up to it, the first job was to get it loaded up. So I roped it up over the back end of the wagon and as it came up over the wagon, up in the air goes the front end of the wagon and I could walk under the front wheels'

'Oh, the girder was a big un was it?' I said.

'Yes,' said Uncle. The curt nod of his head and the look on his face was enough to emphasize the size of it. 'As I roped it on a bit more intending it all to come down quietly, blow me, down comes the front end with a crash and the draw bar of the wagon slams straight into the draw bar on the engine, just right for me to drop the coupling pin in.' Pursing my lips, I let some breath whistle through my teeth to show how astounded I was at such a stroke of luck. 'It all came down with such a crash, I thought I had broke the axle,' he said with a grin.

'After having a look round to make sure everything was alright and tying the girder on I climbed back up on the engine and off we go. After about eighteen miles I reached the bridge, but could not go any further as road and bridge was up, otherwise I would have gone over the bridge to turn round. So I unloaded the girder by the side of the road and as it was a long way to back the engine and wagon to turn round, I hauled back on the reverse lever and backed the wagon through the hedge.'

'Heck, you never did,' said I.

'Yes, and as I made my way off down the road, looking back there was a great glatt [big hole] in the hedge, about this size,' he said, indicating a size with his arms and his shovel.

'Blooming heck, you never did,' I said. 'Did anybody see you?'

'I don't know,' he replied.

'Did you hear about it later on?'

'No, no,' he said.

'Well, it was an awful thing to do.'

'Yes, but I had to get out from there somehow and the hedge would spring back up and a few stakes would pleach it up.

'Well I never,' I said, 'no doubt it was one way of getting out, pity about the hedge.'

'Yes,' he said as we both leant on our shovels and contemplated it for a few minutes.

One gentleman for whom I used to carry out some work was reminded of a story as we sat down together to take our lunch in the kitchen of his old black and white house.

'I went to do some ploughing for a big farmer who lived several miles away. I was all morning ploughing and it was a bitter cold day; there were no cabs on the tractors in those days. I had never worked for this farmer before and about twelve or half past he came down to see how I was getting on. Whereupon he said to me "You're making a good job of this. You come up to the house at dinner time and have some dinner along with us."

'"What time?" I asked.

'"Oh, about one o'clock."

'"Right ho," I said.

'So a little before one I stopped the tractor in order to arrive at the farmhouse at one o'clock. On entering the farmhouse I went into the kitchen, and gosh it was an enormous big room, with the longest kitchen table I had ever seen. Anyway, I washed my hands and was just about to sit down at the table when the farmer stopped me with a "No, no, you sit down here," pointing to a little table in the corner. So I had to sit down at this little table with my back to the farmer and his wife while they enjoyed their dinner at this great table of theirs.

'However, next day ploughing as usual on another bitter cold day, come near one o'clock I made my way up to the farmhouse for dinner, having being asked to do so beforehand by the farmer. Having washed my hands as before, I was just about to sit down at the little table while once again the farmer stopped me saying, "No, no, you sit down here with us," pointing to a place at the big table that had been laid for me. I didn't say anything. I didn't know what to think, I was staggered.

'I don't know to this day how or why the change came about. But what I think happened was, he thought I was just a workman and treated me as such, down very low. He no doubt thought that he was a notch above me. But somehow in that short time he must have found out that my father was a farmer up equal with him. So I came up a notch and I was asked to sit at his table, being that I was a farmer's son. That is what I think happened in order to change his mind. But I don't know for sure. It's only what I think.'

In 1994 I spent a few days working at the Tan House in Brilley, driving there in my van. Pulling into the yard I recalled that my great-grandfather's account book recorded that he was threshing at this very place on 23rd October 1872, and here I was 122 years later on working at the same place. The building and house appeared much as they must have done all those years ago. There was the barn where they would have put the drum and over there the prill where they got the water from for the engine. It looked a very difficult yard to manoeuvre in, but the Old Man knew his stuff. On entering the house, I must have gone into the kitchen where they all sat down to dinner after a morning's threshing.

Going back outside and heaving my tools out of the van I paused by the door casting my eyes over towards the barn and cocking my head on one side and very, very faintly listening into the past, I could hear the humming of the drum.

Going home that night I took in the same panoramic view below as the Old Man would have done. But 'tis now dusk and the lights of the towns, villages and houses are shining out into the night and Hereford with its night-time glow. Aye, it's a modern world now down there.

And so home to tea. To be welcomed by my wife Grace and Mother, and after tea no more to sit down by the fire and talk to Father about old, old days. For he is dead and gone.

Maurice Price's Burrell and threshing drum. Maurice's son Sid is sat on the engine, and Maurice is stood on the drum behind the feeder. Sid used to keep a bottle of wine in a bag hung up on a meat hook on the ceiling, and when Sid was not about, Maurice would sneak a quick sip, topping up the bottle with cold tea. But Sid he always knew when Maurice did this as he always forgot to strain the tea grounds out.

Postscript

In 1957 Father said to me, 'We had better go and get the old Marshall home. She is now a hundred years old, or will be before long.'

'Yes,' I replied, 'let's go'.

So a few days later we made our way down the road to Pentrejack. Alas for those few days' delay, we were too late. Uncle Gwyn had let some scrap men cut her up. Great was our consternation and disappointment, that our grand old engine should meet such an end.

The end of an era: Maurice Price with his Burrell tractor. When Maurice was returning home in the engine, he would sometimes stop at the butcher's to buy some meat, which they would put in a tin in the crank pit on the engine. By the time they reached home the meat would be more or less cooked.

Appendix

Below are a few dates and places taken at random out of the Old Man's Accounts Books for the 1800s, showing the dates he was threshing for farmers in the area around Brilley.

Date	Year	Farmer	Farm
Sat. March 31st	1865	Mr. J. Bromage	Cwmma
Tues. April 4th	1865		Moved to The Cefn
Thurs. April 6th	1865		Moved to Pen Brilley
Oct. 25th	1880		Upper Bridge Court
Feb. 19th	1879	Mr. Lloyd	The Bush
Jan. 1st	1877	Mr. Morgan	Llanshiver
Jan. 3rd	1879	Mr. Bromage	Pen Brilley
Dec. 3rd	1873	Mr. Thomas	Llanhedry
Oct. 23rd	1872	Mr. Hobby	Tan House
Jan. 17th	1874	Mr. Hobby	Pentrecoed
Nov. 3rd	1873	Mr. Price	Pentre Grove
May 8th	1874	Mr. Lloyd	Brilley Green (Building Repairs)
March 25th	1874	Mr. Goodwin	Newchurch
Oct. 10th	1874	Mr. Lewis	The Gaer
Oct. 20th	1873	Mr. Bromage	Cefn
Sept. 3rd	1874	Mr. Evans	Pentrejack
Oct. 9th	1874	Mr. Morris	The Bush
Oct. 13th	1874	Mr. Prothero	Penceste
Oct. 19th	1874	Mr. Price	The Lane
Jan. 19th	1874	?Mr. Mainwaring	Gwernybwch
Dec.	1874	Mr. Price	Court of Hergest
Sept.	1875	Mr. Thomas	Kintley
Sept. 27th	1875	Mr. Knight	Wern

Jan. 1st	1876	Mr. Lloyd	Baynham
Dec. 8th	1876	Mr. Powell	Knapp
Dec. 22nd	1876	Mr. Morgan	Caeau
Dec. 19th	1876	Mr. Morgan	Pontvaen
Dec. 28th	1876	Mr. Owen	Tynycwm
Feb. 13th	1877	Mr. Dew	Bridge of Almeley
Aug. 20th	1877	Mr. James Saveker	
Mon. Jan. 2nd to Thurs. Jan. 5th	1865	Repairing the machine, bending and turning a shaker crank and fitting crankshaft in machine	
Fri. Jan. 6th	1865	Mr. Canope	Welson
Sat. Jan. 7th	1865		Moving to Kintley Barn
Fri. Jan. 20th	1865		Moving to Banks of Pleasure
Sat. Jan. 21st	1865		Threshing at Banks of Pleasure
Jan. 12th	1865	Mr. R. Thomas	Kintley
Jan. 13th	1865	Mr. R. Thomas	Court of Brilley
Jan. 14th	1865	Mr. Davies	Llanhedry
Jan. 21st	1865	Mr. Bromage	Threshing at Banks of Pleasure
Feb. 9th	1865	Mr. T. Powell	Lane of Brilley
March	1865	Mr. Bromage	Cwmma
Nov. 17th	1869	Mr. Stokes	Sunnybank
Sept. 13th	1880	Mrs. Perry Herrick	Pentrecoed
Oct.	1880	Mr. James	The Castle, Crowthers Pool
Dec. 13th	1881	Mr. Thomas	Holborn
	1874	Mr. Morgan	Redborough
Nov. 11th	1878	Mr. Davey Lloyd	Banks of Pleasure
Oct. 15th	1874	Mr. Thomas	The Court
March	1882	Mr. Hobby	Tan House
March	1882	Mr. Price	Pentregrove
March	1882	Mr. Mainwaring	The Cefn
March	1882	Mr. Hobby	Hengoed
March	1882	Mr. Meredith	The Apostles
March	1882	Mr. Hobby	Pentremiley
March 7th	1882		Sunnybank

A few dates and places taken at random from the Account Books for the 1900s:

Date	Year	Farmer	Farm
Sept. 15th	1908	Mr. Hughes	Madley
Jan. 11th	1908	Mr. Morgan	Llanhedry
Nov. 20th	1907	Mr. Hobby	Hengoed
Oct. 2nd	1905	Mr. Lloyd	The Camp (Perhaps the Camp Field along the Apostles Lane. It is known that they threshed there)
Sept. 29th	1905	Mr. Jones	Tuck Mill
March 20th	1908	Mr Prosser	Brilley Court

Also from Logaston Press

Herefordshire Folklore
by Roy Palmer
Paperback, 230 pages, copiously illustrated   £12.95

Roy Palmer presents the folklore of the county as a series of themes that embrace landscape, buildings, beliefs, work, seasons and people. In so doing, ten chapters are crafted that can stand alone or be read as a whole, each full of snippets of insight into the county's past in a way that adds to anyone's enjoyment of Herefordshire.

The Folklore of Radnorshire
by Roy Palmer
Paperback, 272 pages, over 100 black and white illustrations   £12.95

Roy Palmer weaves the folklore of the old county into a seamless whole, where ancient spirits, half-remembered tales, traditions handed down over the centuries, acts of pranksters, inexplicable events, and stories that leave one wondering at the truth, are brought together to create a vibrant view of Radnorshire and its beliefs and customs. Illustrated with a mixture of old and current photographs, drawings, ballad sheets and music samples, this is a book you can choose either to dip into or settle down to read from cover to cover.

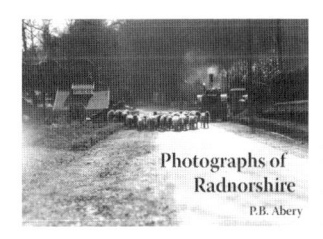

Photographs of Radnorshire
by P.B. Abery
Paperback, 72 pages, 60 black and white photographs   £4.95

Abery captured a way of life, recording events and activities throughout Mid-Wales and the Border Counties during the first half of the twentieth century. This book is a collection of his photographs of Radnorshire and illustrates the towns, villages, social life, people and landscape of the county.

Merrily's Border:
The Marches share their secrets
with novelist Phil Rickman & photographer John Mason
112 pages with over 90 colour and 60 black and white photographs
Hardback £20   Paperback £12.95

A land where ancient mystery is never far below the surface: the Knights Templar and the Green Man; the secret lore of apples; the lair of the real Hound of the Baskervilles; a pentagram of churches; a serial killer's dark legacy; Edward Elgar and Alfred Watkins, discoverer of ley-lines. With its blend of crime and the paranormal, Phil Rickman's addictive Merrily Watkins series about the diocesan exorcist for Hereford has virtually established a new fictional genre. But the fiction is never far from an often surprising and occasionally disturbing reality. All the novels are set in actual locations along the Welsh Border, with real history – recent and ancient – and indigenous folklore. Revealing the sources and the inspiration, this book takes readers to the heart of it all.

Also from Logaston Press

Brilley Voices
by Brilley Living Archive Group
Paperback, 128 pages, 100 black & white illustrations   £10

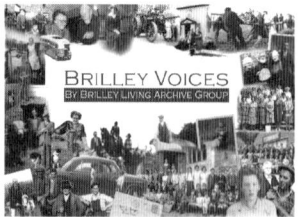

The two parishes of Brilley and Michaelchurch lie one on either side of the English/Welsh border, but share a village hall and have joined hands in many community projects. This book is a selection of residents' memories, accompanied by photographs, which portray a community that has gently changed over time, not least through the loss of the village school and a gradual reduction in the number of people whose livelihood depends upon agriculture, but yet clearly retains a certain vibrancy. Within these pages are tales of school and farm life down the years, of many characters who have come and gone, of a wartime factory and Kington Camp.

Roses round the door?
Rural images, realities & responses: Herefordshire, 1830s-1930s
by Tim Ward
Paperback, 168 pages with 135 black and white illustrations   £12.95

Tim Ward's collection of postcards includes many images of Herefordshire's past rural life: harvesting and hop-picking, cidermaking and cattle breeding, blacksmiths, beekeepers and basketmakers. Behind these photographs, carefully posed as most of them had to be for the slow business of early photography, were the working lives of men and women – and many of those lives were a hard struggle, however picturesque the scenes seem to be. Life was far from a 'roses round the door' country idyll. Dispossessed by the Enclosure Acts that took common land from rural people and forced them into miserable working and living conditions, Herefordshire's agricultural labourers eventually found a voice, with the formation, from 1871, of a succession of farmworkers' unions. Tim Ward charts the history of the unions, the strong characters who founded them, including Thomas Strange, William Gibson Ward, Joseph Arch and Sidney Box, and what became of their attempts to bring about change.

Herefordshire Place-Names
by Bruce Coplestone-Crow
Paperback, 268 pages with 7 maps   £12.95

This book seeks to explain the place-names of Herefordshire – not just those of the major settlements, but also of districts, hamlets and even old farmsteads. There is often additional information about the family which may have lent its name to the place, why a name has changed over time or concerning old charter bounds. At the beginning of the book the author has used his considerable knowledge to set out in some detail the origins for the old district names within Herefordshire, many of which (such as Archenfield, Leen, Lyde, Maund and Straddle) are a component of many current place-names.